Probability of Doom:

Humanity at the Crossroads of Artificial Intelligence

Lucas Hartwell

Lucas Hartwell

Copyright 2024 Lucas Hartwell. All Rights reserved. No part of this publication may be reproduced without the consent of the author.

"If arithmetical skill is the measure of intelligence, then computers have been more intelligent than all human beings all along. If the ability to play chess is the measure, then there are computers now in existence that are more intelligent than any but a very few human beings.

However, if insight, intuition, creativity, the ability to view a problem as a whole and guess the answer by the "feel" of the situation, is a measure of intelligence, computers are very unintelligent indeed. Nor can we see right now how this deficiency in computers can be easily remedied, since human beings cannot program a computer to be intuitive or creative for the very good reason that we do not know what we ourselves do when we exercise these qualities."

— Isaac Asimov

Lucas Hartwell

Table of Contents

Chapter 1: The Dawn of a New Era

Chapter 2: The Trajectory of Human Progress

Chapter 3: The Utopian Vision

Chapter 4: The Shadow of Doom

Chapter 5: The Economic Earthquake

Chapter 6: Decision Time—Humanity's Choice

Chapter 7: Global Implications

Chapter 8: Technological Restraint vs. Progress

Chapter 9: Preparing for the Unknown

Chapter 10: Embracing the Future

Introduction

The world is changing at a breakneck pace, and at the heart of this transformation lies artificial intelligence. From the moment you wake up to the smart alarm on your phone to the personalized recommendations in your social media feed, AI is quietly shaping our daily lives. But its impact stretches far beyond these everyday conveniences.

Imagine a world where diseases are diagnosed before symptoms appear, where traffic flows seamlessly through smart city grids, and where communication barriers between languages dissolve in real-time. This isn't science fiction—it's the world AI is creating right now.

Yet, as we stand on the cusp of this technological revolution, we must also confront its shadows. What happens when AI algorithms make life-altering decisions about our healthcare, our jobs, or our legal system? How do we ensure that the benefits of AI are distributed equitably across society? And perhaps most crucially, how do we maintain control over systems that may one day surpass human intelligence?

"Probability of Doom" isn't just a book—it's an invitation to engage with one of the most pressing issues of our time. Through stories of innovation and cautionary tales, we'll explore the intricate web of AI's influence on our world. From the labs of Silicon Valley to the streets of developing nations, we'll meet the people at the forefront of this revolution and those grappling with its consequences.

As we journey through these pages, we'll arm ourselves with the knowledge to navigate this new landscape. We'll learn to see beyond the hype and fear-mongering, to understand the real potential and genuine risks of AI. This book is your guide to becoming an informed advocate for responsible AI development, empowering you to shape the future we're racing towards.

The dawn of AI is here. The question is: are we ready for it?

Lucas Hartwell

Chapter 1: The Dawn of a New Era

A Turning Point in History

Throughout human history, there have been key moments that have changed the way we live. From discovering fire to creating the wheel, each breakthrough has brought about significant changes that have pushed societies into new ways of thinking and existing. Right now, we are on the edge of another big change: the rise of artificial intelligence (AI). With each day that goes by, this exciting new technology is starting to reshape our world in ways that once seemed like something out of a science fiction story. As we find ourselves at this important crossroads in history, it's important to grasp how deeply AI will impact our lives—both the good and the bad.

Artificial intelligence is much more than just a new gadget; it's a mirror reflecting humanity's endless desire to innovate. This desire can be traced back to our earliest ancestors, who learned to use the power of nature to enhance their lives. Today, we're using that same creativity to build machines that can learn, adapt, and even think. This shift from using simple tools to working alongside intelligent machines marks a significant change that brings up just as many questions as it does answers. What does it mean to share our world with creations that might think faster than we do? How do we find a balance between the potential for progress and the risks that come with it?

To really appreciate this new chapter, we need to first understand what artificial intelligence really is. Many people have misunderstandings about AI—thanks in part to movies, books, and media that often depict it as an all-knowing force. In reality, AI is a branch of study focused on creating systems that can perform tasks usually needing human intelligence. These tasks include learning from experience, recognizing patterns, and making decisions based on data. However, the power of AI isn't limitless; it's shaped by the algorithms and data that fuel its growth. The idea that machines will eventually surpass human intelligence in every way is both fascinating and frightening, but it's not something we need to worry about right now.

When we look at what AI can do, it becomes clear that these systems rely heavily on human input. They learn from the information we provide, mirroring our values, biases, and choices. This teamwork raises important questions about who's responsible when things go wrong. If an AI system makes a harmful decision, who should be held accountable? The programmer? The user? The machine itself? Working through these questions is key to understanding how AI will develop and fit into our lives.

As AI continues to grow, our relationship with machines is changing. We are no longer just users of tools; we are entering into a partnership where AI helps enhance our skills and enriches our experiences. Take a look at how AI is already improving various fields like healthcare, finance, transportation, and education. In healthcare, AI algorithms help doctors diagnose diseases by analyzing medical images more accurately than the human eye alone. In finance, machine learning tools sift through large amounts of data to find patterns that can inform investment strategies. These examples show how AI can enhance human abilities and improve our quality of life.

But this partnership comes with its own set of challenges. The rise of AI brings up worries about job loss, privacy, and security. As machines take over more tasks that humans used to do, the job market is experiencing disruptions that push people to adapt and learn new skills. The fear of becoming obsolete is very real, sparking debates about the future of employment and what skills we will need in a more automated world. Additionally, as AI becomes more integrated into our daily lives, it gathers and analyzes huge amounts of personal data, raising concerns about privacy and surveillance. How do we protect our rights and freedoms in a world where we are always connected and under constant observation?

These challenges highlight the need for a strong framework to guide the development and use of AI. It's essential that we work together—technologists, ethicists, policymakers, and the public—to ensure AI serves the common good. This conversation should focus on transparency, accountability, and inclusivity, creating a space where all voices are heard in shaping the technology that will influence our future. It's crucial that we find our way through this landscape together, making the most of AI's potential while keeping an eye on its risks.

Looking back at this moment in history, we should consider the lessons we've learned from the past. Technological advancements often move faster than our ethical and regulatory responses, resulting in unexpected consequences. From the Industrial Revolution to the rise of the internet, we have repeatedly faced the societal impacts of our innovations. We now have the chance to learn from those experiences and apply those lessons to AI development.

The conversation about AI isn't just about the technology itself; it's about the kind of society we want to build. Are we ready to chase progress at any cost, or will we take a more thoughtful approach, weighing the benefits alongside the risks? The stakes are incredibly high, and the decisions we make today will influence the path of our civilization for years to come.

It's crucial to foster a culture of informed discussion about artificial intelligence. This isn't just a job for experts; it's a responsibility we all share as engaged citizens. To effectively navigate the complexities of AI, we need to understand the technology, its effects, and our role in shaping its future. This means promoting education and conversations that clarify what AI can really do, encouraging a broader understanding that goes beyond sensationalized stories.

In this new era, we find ourselves at a crucial juncture, faced with choices that will steer the course of human progress. Will we confidently step into the future, embracing all the possibilities AI offers, or will we proceed cautiously, aware of the uncertainties ahead? The answer lies not only in technological progress but also in our shared values and ethical considerations. As caretakers of this powerful transformation, we must be aware of the legacy we create for future generations, ensuring that AI is developed and used in a responsible and ethical way.

The story of artificial intelligence is one of teamwork, challenge, and opportunity. As we think about this moment in history, let's commit to engaging thoughtfully with the implications of AI, working towards a future where technology enhances our human experience rather than diminishes it. The choices we make now will not only shape our relationship with machines but will ultimately define what it means to be human in a rapidly changing world.

AI Unveiled

Artificial intelligence, or AI, has become a hot topic that sparks conversations in boardrooms, classrooms, and coffee shops everywhere. But what exactly is this phenomenon that has captured so many people's attention? For most of us, AI might seem like a mysterious concept, often shown in exciting science fiction stories. However, the truth is much more intriguing. AI isn't some all-knowing entity; it's actually a collection of advanced tools designed to carry out specific tasks by using data to guide decisions and actions. Understanding AI helps clear up the confusion, breaking it down into parts that highlight not only what it can do but also where it falls short.

Think about a child learning to recognize animals. At first, a little one might see a dog and mistakenly call it a cat simply because they haven't learned the difference yet. But after they see more animals, get corrected, and have patient guidance from a parent, they start to grasp the subtle differences. This learning process is similar to machine learning, which is a key piece of AI. In machine learning, algorithms are like that curious child. They learn from data and past experiences to get better over time. Just as our young learner asks questions and absorbs information, machine learning systems adjust their answers based on input, refining their understanding of tasks as they go.

Now, let's switch gears to natural language processing (NLP). Have you ever chatted with a virtual assistant, asking it to set an alarm or play your favorite song? That smooth interaction happens thanks to NLP, a part of AI that helps machines understand and respond to human language. Imagine teaching a toddler to speak. Initially, their sounds are jumbled, but as they hear more words, they start forming sentences and grasping meanings. NLP is all about training algorithms to recognize patterns in language—like grammar, meaning, and context—so they can create responses that sound human-like. But remember, these tools don't "understand" language like we do. They analyze and predict based on patterns and data, often generating responses that sound sensible but lack true comprehension.

Next up are neural networks, an important part of AI that mimics how our brains process information. Picture a web of interconnected nodes, similar to a spider's intricate web. Each connection is like a pathway for data, resembling the synapses in our brains that send signals. Neural networks learn by adjusting the strengths of these connections based on incoming data. When they're being trained, they essentially fine-tune themselves to improve their output, just like a musician practices to get better at their craft. This is why neural networks work so well for tasks like image recognition, where they can sift through thousands of images to spot features and patterns. In the end, they can recognize a cat, even if they've never encountered that particular cat before.

Even with all the thrilling advancements in AI, there are still myths that cloud public understanding. One common misconception is that AI will eventually outsmart human intelligence. While that idea makes for a great movie plot—complete with dramatic music—it's important to clarify that AI operates strictly within the limits of its programming and the data it's trained on. AI lacks consciousness, emotions, and the intuitive insights that define human thinking. So while it may excel at specific tasks like quickly analyzing huge amounts of data, it does so without any real understanding or awareness. This highlights that AI isn't meant to replace human intelligence; rather, it's a tool designed to boost our abilities.

Let's take a look at some everyday examples of AI you might encounter in your daily life. For instance, streaming services like

Netflix and Spotify use recommendation systems powered by AI to suggest content you might enjoy. Ever wonder how they seem to know exactly what you want to watch or listen to? It's not magic; it's algorithms studying your viewing habits, comparing them to those of other users with similar tastes, and crafting a personalized list just for you. This is a clear example of AI enhancing your experience based on data-driven insights.

On our smartphones, virtual assistants like Siri and Google Assistant have become well-known companions. How do these digital helpers understand our commands? Through the intricate mechanisms of NLP, they process spoken language and respond with pre-programmed answers or actions. What's impressive is how they learn over time, adapting to the way you phrase requests and even picking up on your preferences. Again, this isn't about the machine having a consciousness to understand your needs; it's about analyzing tons of data to provide the best responses.

While it's easy to get excited about what AI can do, it's just as important to recognize the challenges that come along with it. As AI systems continue to grow and change, they raise serious ethical questions. For instance, who is responsible when an AI makes a mistake? Imagine relying on an AI to drive your car, and it gets into an accident. Is it the manufacturer's fault, the software developer's, or just an odd glitch in the machine? Figuring out responsibility in such situations requires careful thought and open discussions among tech experts, lawmakers, and society as a whole.

Another challenge is the potential for bias in AI. Because AI systems learn from the data we give them, they can unintentionally adopt the human biases present in that data. This could lead to unfair treatment in areas like hiring or law enforcement, where AI is increasingly used to assist in decision-making. Therefore, it's crucial to use diverse and representative datasets when training AI to reduce the risk of reinforcing social inequalities.

As we navigate through this complex landscape, the need for strong ethical guidelines becomes more pressing. The development of AI shouldn't happen in a bubble; it should involve collaboration among tech developers, ethicists, policymakers, and the public. Transparency about how AI systems work, accountability for their results, and including a variety of voices in decision-making processes are all vital parts of building trust in AI technologies.

Reflecting on our interactions with technology shows that we need a deeper understanding of AI. This isn't just a talk for tech experts; it's a shared responsibility for everyone. We should educate ourselves about AI's capabilities and limitations and engage in conversations that encourage a clearer understanding of its impact on society.

The story of artificial intelligence is still unfolding, and as part of this story, we have a unique chance to shape its future. Will we embrace AI to empower ourselves, or will we let fear and misunderstanding guide our approach? Think about the choices we face: a future where AI enriches our lives or one where it remains a source of worry and confusion. The direction we take will not only affect our relationship with technology but also define what it means to be human in a world increasingly connected to artificial intelligence.

As we stand at this exciting crossroads, it's crucial to engage thoughtfully with the technological advancements around us. AI has the power to improve many aspects of our lives, but it's up to us to make sure that it's used ethically and responsibly. The challenges we face today will shape the world for future generations, and our choices will resonate well into the future.

In this ever-changing environment, the value of informed discussions can't be stressed enough. We have the power to steer AI development in ways that reflect our values and hopes. By nurturing a culture of understanding, teamwork, and ethical thinking, we can create an environment where AI serves as a powerful tool that brings us closer together, enhancing human experience instead of overshadowing it.

As we move ahead, let's remain mindful guardians of this transformative technology, ensuring that AI evolves alongside human needs and dreams. The choices we make today will define the legacy we leave for tomorrow, making it crucial to approach the rise of AI with both enthusiasm and caution. By doing so, we can foster a future where technology complements our humanity, enriching our lives and paving the way for a better world for everyone.

From Tools to Partners

The relationship between humanity and artificial intelligence has changed a lot over the years. At first, we saw AI mainly as a tool—kind of like a super calculator that could handle tasks that were too boring or complicated for us to do by ourselves. But now, as AI has grown and improved, we're starting to view it as a partner we can work with in many areas of our lives. This isn't just about changing how we talk about technology; it's a big shift in how we think about it, how we see its role in our lives, and how we picture our future together.

Picture a world where AI isn't just some cold, distant program running in a data center but a helpful companion that boosts our skills and creativity in amazing ways. In healthcare, for example, AI can help doctors make more accurate diagnoses by quickly analyzing huge amounts of medical data that would take a human forever to sift through. In finance, AI is becoming an important part of the decision-making process, giving human analysts insights that help them navigate a complex market. And in the world of creativity, AI is stepping in to help artists, writers, and musicians, sparking new ideas and enhancing their creative journeys in ways they might never have thought of.

Let's dive deeper into healthcare, where AI is making a real difference in diagnostics. Traditionally, diagnosing diseases was a long and often tedious task. Doctors would spend hours going through patient histories, lab results, and medical research to come to their best conclusions. But now, AI can analyze enormous datasets in real-time. A great example is IBM's Watson, which famously won on the quiz show "Jeopardy!" and has since shifted its focus to medicine. Watson can scan medical literature, compare it with patient data, and suggest treatment options tailored to individual patients—all in just seconds.

Imagine a doctor facing a patient with a complex mix of symptoms. Instead of relying solely on their own knowledge, they can turn to an AI that has examined millions of similar cases. The AI might propose possible diagnoses the doctor hadn't thought of or point out the newest treatment options based on the latest research. This teamwork helps healthcare professionals work with greater confidence and accuracy, leading to better outcomes for patients. In situations where every second counts, this kind of collaboration can truly save lives.

In finance, AI's role keeps growing, playing a critical part in everything from assessing risk to making trading decisions. In the past, financial analysts would spend countless hours combing through spreadsheets, looking for trends, and analyzing market data to inform their choices. Now, AI can process this information at lightning speed, spotting patterns and anomalies that might go unnoticed otherwise. Companies like BlackRock and Goldman Sachs are already using AI to refine their investment strategies and reduce risks, employing machine learning to analyze past data and forecast future market trends.

Imagine an investment analyst working hand-in-hand with a powerful AI model. The analyst can still rely on their own instincts and market experience, but now they have a capable partner that provides data-driven insights, allowing them to make choices with a wider perspective. This teamwork not only boosts the accuracy of financial predictions but also encourages a culture of innovation, as humans and machines learn from one another in a cycle of continuous improvement.

Even in the creative arts, often viewed as a purely human domain, AI is stepping in as a collaborator rather than a competitor. Take music composition, for instance. AI programs can analyze thousands of songs across different genres, learning patterns and styles to create their own tunes. This partnership extends beyond just the algorithm producing a melody; it involves musicians using AI-generated music as inspiration to spark new ideas.

Think about a songwriter who's feeling stuck and can't find inspiration for their next track. Instead of staring blankly at a page, they might turn to an AI that generates melodies or lyrics aligned with the themes and styles they love. This partnership can lead to innovative music that combines human emotion with AI's analytical flair, resulting in a final piece that neither could have created alone. We're pushing the limits of creativity, and in that process, we're redefining what it means to be an artist today.

However, with this shift from seeing AI as a mere tool to recognizing it as a partner comes a lot of ethical questions we need to think about. The more we rely on AI in critical areas like healthcare, finance, and creative expression, the more accountable we must be to ensure these systems are built and used properly. Issues like transparency, accountability, and the risk of bias in AI systems are just a few of the important challenges that need our attention.

One major concern is the possibility of bias. AI systems learn from historical data, and if that data carries existing prejudices—based on race, gender, or socioeconomic status—AI can end up perpetuating and even worsening these biases in its decisions. For example, if an AI used for hiring is trained on past employment data that favors certain demographics, it may unintentionally disadvantage equally qualified candidates from other backgrounds.

This highlights the need for diverse and representative datasets when training AI to minimize biased outcomes. We can't just focus on creating advanced algorithms; we also need to make sure they are built on a foundation of fairness and inclusivity. It's up to developers, policymakers, and all of us to engage in discussions about the ethical implications of AI and to establish guidelines that encourage responsible practices.

Another ethical issue is accountability. When an AI system makes a mistake—like a misdiagnosis that negatively affects a patient—who should be held responsible? Is it the developers who designed the algorithm, the healthcare providers who trusted it, or the organization that used the technology? These aren't just theoretical questions; they need serious consideration as we rely more on AI. Creating clear rules and frameworks for accountability can help us navigate these tricky situations and ensure there are ways to address and fix the harm done when AI fails.

As we think about the future, it's vital that we create a sense of shared responsibility in our relationship with AI. We need to see ourselves as active participants in the ongoing conversation about the ethical development of AI, not just passive bystanders waiting to see what happens. This means getting involved with the issues at stake, advocating for transparency in AI processes, and pushing for accountability when things go wrong.

The fast-paced evolution of AI challenges not just our ethical standards but also how we understand what it means to be human. As machines become better at doing tasks we once considered uniquely human, we have to think about what that means for our identity and society. What will it look like when AI doesn't just assist us but also enhances our thinking and creativity? Will we still view ourselves as the main decision-makers in our lives, or will we start to see our actions as just reactions to what an algorithm tells us?

The key to keeping our humanity in this partnership is to embrace collaboration instead of fearing it. By seeing AI as an extension of our abilities rather than a replacement, we can build a future where technology makes our lives better, boosting our strengths instead of taking away our roles. As we move forward, it's crucial that we cultivate a culture of responsible AI development—one that prioritizes ethical considerations and highlights the importance of human oversight.

The journey from viewing AI as just a tool to recognizing it as a partner is filled with both exciting opportunities and significant challenges. As we explore the possibilities of AI in healthcare, finance, and the arts, we must stay mindful of the ethical implications that come with this partnership. By encouraging discussions that include a variety of viewpoints and prioritize transparency and accountability, we can work toward a future where AI truly enhances human abilities and enriches our shared experience.

The choices we make today will shape the path of AI development, influencing not only how we interact with technology but also how we perceive our roles in a more complex world. Let's welcome this partnership with open hearts and minds, understanding that the connection between human intelligence and artificial intelligence can open new doors for creativity, innovation, and understanding. Together, we can create a future where AI is not just a tool we use but a trusted partner in our shared journey.

Chapter 2: The Trajectory of Human Progress

Milestones of Innovation

The story of human progress is an incredible journey filled with breakthroughs that have not only changed societies but also transformed how we connect with the world around us. From the first spark of creativity that inspired our ancestors to make basic tools from stone to the complex algorithms that drive our modern lives, each innovation has pushed us forward. By taking a closer look at these milestones, we can better appreciate the amazing advancements we are seeing today, especially in the world of artificial intelligence.

Imagine the early days of humanity: a time when survival relied on the ability to create and use tools. The invention of the wheel, a seemingly simple circular object, marked a huge turning point in human capability. This innovation didn't just make transportation easier; it changed trade, agriculture, and warfare in profound ways. Without the wheel, the migrations of ancient people would have been vastly different, trade routes would have stayed basic, and the rise and fall of empires would have happened at a much slower pace. The wheel became the foundation upon which industries were built and civilizations flourished.

As we journey through history, let's consider the rise of writing systems. From the cuneiform tablets of Mesopotamia to the hieroglyphics of ancient Egypt, the ability to write down thoughts, transactions, and stories fundamentally changed how we interacted with one another. Writing allowed knowledge to be passed down through generations, making education possible and helping to create laws. In a way, it was the first step toward collective memory, allowing societies to learn from their past and plan for their futures. This innovation set the stage for the complex social systems and cultural identities we recognize today.

Fast forward to the Scientific Revolution of the 16th and 17th centuries. This era was marked by a fantastic mix of ideas and discoveries that reshaped our understanding of the universe. Think of pioneers like Galileo, Newton, and Kepler, who bravely questioned long-held beliefs and used the scientific method—an innovation in itself—to uncover the laws of nature. The impact of this revolution was immense; it provided the intellectual foundation that would spark technological advancements and eventually lead to the Industrial Revolution.

The Industrial Revolution, one of the most transformative milestones in human history, brought about an era of machines. The introduction of steam engines, spinning jennies, and power looms completely changed labor and production. No longer were people solely dependent on manual labor; machines began to take the spotlight. This shift not only boosted efficiency and productivity but also sparked urbanization, as people moved to cities in search of jobs. The Industrial Revolution fundamentally altered society, creating new social classes and changing traditional ways of life.

Next came the arrival of electricity, a milestone that lit up the modern world. Harnessing electrical energy transformed industries, homes, and communication. Innovations like the telegraph and telephone changed how quickly we could share information, shrinking the world and bringing people closer. Letters that once took weeks to arrive could now be sent in an instant across vast distances. Electricity became the lifeblood of modern civilization, enabling new innovations that paved the way for the digital age.

As we wrap up our historical overview, we can't overlook the rise of computing technology. The invention of the first computers in the mid-20th century marked another significant turn in our story of innovation. These machines, initially created for complex calculations, grew into powerful devices capable of performing billions of operations in the blink of an eye. The development of the internet later in the century opened up a whole new world of communication and information sharing, leading to a level of global connectivity we had never experienced before.

The internet, the exciting culmination of earlier innovations, has transformed nearly every aspect of our lives. It has changed how we do business, share knowledge, and even how we connect with friends and family. The barriers that once kept nations and cultures apart have begun to fade, allowing information to flow freely and connecting people across continents. In many ways, the internet acts as a metaphorical bridge, enabling humanity to collectively tap into the vast pool of knowledge and creativity available around the globe.

Now, as we look toward the next chapter of human progress, artificial intelligence stands out as both a result of these incredible milestones and a driving force for future advancements. The rise of AI is a natural extension of centuries of innovation, following the journey from the wheel to the internet and beyond. This technology isn't just a tool; it's a partner that can enhance human potential in ways that once felt like science fiction.

Reflecting on these milestones, it's clear that innovation is a core part of being human. Each breakthrough builds on the last, creating a complex web of advancements that push civilization forward. The path of human progress is a fascinating mix of creativity, necessity, and curiosity, a story that continues to develop in our present day. With every leap in innovation, we're reminded that our journey isn't finished; the next chapter of human progress is being written right now.

The excitement surrounding artificial intelligence is contagious, as it promises to revolutionize industries, tackle global challenges, and improve our daily lives. However, as we welcome these advancements, we must also remember the lessons learned from our past. Each milestone of innovation carries both potential and challenges—offering the chance to uplift humanity while also posing ethical questions. As we move forward, it's up to us to navigate this new landscape with care, ensuring that our progress aligns with the values and dreams we hold dear.

In the next section, we will explore how the rapid changes brought on by AI are not only part of this extraordinary history but also reshaping the very essence of innovation itself. The speed of change we're experiencing is unlike anything before, and understanding its implications will be vital for shaping our shared future.

The Acceleration of Change

We're at the beginning of a new era, one that's buzzing with rapid technological growth, and artificial intelligence is at the forefront, making waves like never before. The spark ignited by earlier innovations has turned into a blazing fire, pushing us into a time where change is happening faster than we could have imagined. AI stands out in this mix, evolving in ways that seem almost magical. It learns from vast amounts of data, constantly improving and adapting. We are witnessing an exciting shift where breakthroughs are happening so quickly, it feels like innovation is happening right before our eyes.

    One of the most thrilling things about AI is how fast it develops. The idea that machines can learn without the same limitations that humans have is both fascinating and a bit intimidating. Take smartphones, for instance. They first hit the market in the early 2000s and have undergone countless upgrades since then. Now, imagine a technology that doesn't just improve gradually but learns and adapts to what users need in real-time. This is what AI does—it's a game changer that finds solutions at lightning speed, leaving even the most experienced tech experts amazed.

    Just like the wheel transformed travel, AI is set to change industries across the board. It's not just speeding up evolution; it's also working hand-in-hand with other cutting-edge technologies. Think about a future where AI seamlessly connects with biotechnology, quantum computing, and renewable energy. These areas were already advancing quickly on their own, but AI has come along and created a powerful synergy that takes progress to dizzying new heights. The blending of these fields isn't just a coincidence; it's a dynamic force that enhances the capabilities of each technology involved.

Consider biotechnology for a moment. The fusion of AI and genetic engineering has led to groundbreaking developments in medicine. Algorithms can sift through genetic information faster than any human could, identifying mutations and possible treatments with stunning efficiency. This means we can navigate the road to personalized medicine more quickly, unlocking mysteries about diseases at a speed we couldn't have dreamed of before. These breakthroughs aren't just ideas; they promise to change healthcare and make life-saving treatments available to more people than ever.

Meanwhile, in the world of quantum computing, AI is finding new ways to thrive. Imagine the possibilities of quantum AI—the ability to analyze information at incredible speeds, solving tough problems from climate change to financial predictions. The collaboration between AI and quantum mechanics is on the verge of changing how we understand computation itself, offering solutions to challenges that have haunted us for ages. This connection between technologies shows us that innovation thrives on teamwork and collaboration.

The automotive industry is also feeling the revolutionary impact of AI, especially as we move towards self-driving cars. The power to process and learn from huge amounts of real-time data has made transportation safer and more efficient. Companies are no longer just making cars; they are creating intelligent systems that learn from how people drive, understand road conditions, and analyze traffic patterns. The effects of this change are enormous—fewer accidents, lower emissions, and improved city travel are just the beginning. But the transformation doesn't end there; it spreads to related industries like insurance and city planning, making us rethink how we live our everyday lives.

However, as we welcome this change, we also need to face the challenges that come with such rapid progress. While there are plenty of opportunities for innovation, there are also worries about job loss and ethical issues surrounding AI decisions. The story of progress isn't just about the technologies that succeed; it's also about the people whose lives are affected by these changes.

The fear of AI taking over jobs has sparked a lot of important discussions, and for good reason. Entire industries might face major shifts, leading to job losses that can make many feel uncertain about their futures. But it's important to see this disruption as a chance for new opportunities as well. Historically, when new technologies emerge, they often create new jobs even as they make some old ones disappear. The real challenge today is not just about dealing with job loss but also about retraining and equipping people to step into new roles. This calls on society to focus on education and ongoing learning, making sure the workforce has the skills needed to thrive in a future that includes AI.

Additionally, the ethical questions surrounding AI technologies are significant and require careful thought. As machines take on decision-making in areas like healthcare, law, and policing, accountability becomes a major concern. When an AI makes a mistake, who is responsible? How can we guarantee that these systems are fair and unbiased? These aren't just theoretical debates; they are urgent issues that need proper regulations and ethical guidelines to ensure that technology develops responsibly.

The need for suitable regulations is even clearer when we consider the societal effects of AI. With great power comes great responsibility, and as we harness these advanced technologies, we must also nurture a culture of accountability and transparency. It's crucial to involve a variety of voices—scientists, ethicists, lawmakers, and the public—in conversations that will shape AI's future. Our goal should be to create an environment where creativity can thrive while still respecting human rights and ethical values.

As the world increasingly turns to AI to solve tough problems, the weight of our responsibility grows. From tackling climate change to addressing social inequality, AI's applications are wide-reaching and impactful. We are at a turning point where actively engaging with these technologies can lead to solutions that benefit all of humanity. We have the power to advocate for advancements that not only focus on efficiency and profit but also align with the values we care about deeply.

In this fast-changing technological landscape, it's vital to cultivate a mindset that acknowledges both the uplifting potential of innovation and its capacity to disrupt. As we make our way through this journey, the need for informed advocacy and thoughtful reflection becomes clear. The lessons we've learned from the past should guide our actions, reminding us that progress isn't always a straightforward path; it requires careful guidance.

As we think about what an AI-driven future might look like, we find ourselves in a unique position. The rapid pace of change is remarkable, marked by the blending of technologies, shifts in established norms, and the urgent need for ethical considerations. We need to channel this momentum not just for our own benefit but for the generations to come, making sure the innovations we support today lead us to a future that reflects our best values.

The story of this acceleration is still being written, with new chapters unfolding daily. It's up to us to engage with thoughtfulness, push for responsible practices, and make sure that the incredible power of AI becomes a force for good. By embracing this challenge, we can navigate the complexities of a swiftly changing world and become empowered to shape a brighter future for everyone.

The Singularity Horizon

As the sun sets on the world we know, we look ahead—not at the fading light of the day, but at the dazzling glow of technological progress. The idea of the Singularity captures our imagination, serving as a symbol of both excitement and concern. It's a moment where our creativity meets the intelligence of machines, creating new possibilities that could change everything we thought we knew. The Singularity is often described as the point when artificial intelligence outsmarts human intelligence, marking a huge shift in how we live. This is when the machines we've built might start to enhance and even create themselves, evolving in ways we can't fully grasp.

Throughout history, there have been key moments that have changed the course of humanity—discoveries that opened doors to new ways of living. The discovery of fire changed how we interacted with nature, the invention of the wheel gave us freedom to travel, and the rise of the internet transformed how we share information. Each of these breakthroughs sparked hope for a future filled with potential. However, with every advancement, society has had to face the challenges that came with them. The Singularity represents our next great leap, but it also brings a lot of unanswered questions. What happens when machines can think and learn on their own? How do we decide what's right or wrong in this new world?

To understand the Singularity better, we need to look at how artificial intelligence has developed over the years. From its early ideas in the mid-20th century to becoming a part of our everyday lives today, AI has evolved significantly. The advanced algorithms we have now allow machines to learn, adapt, and predict outcomes with remarkable accuracy. This isn't just a far-off dream; it's happening right now, reshaping industries and changing what it means to be human.

But as we stand on the edge of this new frontier, it's important to remember that not every advancement is purely good. While AI has the potential to greatly boost human abilities, there's also the risk of it being misused in ways that could have serious consequences. This becomes even more critical when we think about a future where AI can make decisions all on its own. In such a scenario, who will be in charge? If machines start to think independently, will their goals align with our values, or will they follow their own paths?

The promise of the Singularity is tempting: a time when diseases could be wiped out, poverty eliminated, and the secrets of the universe uncovered by superintelligent machines designed to help us. Imagine AI systems that use vast amounts of data to create personalized medicine, develop green energy solutions, and invent new technologies. In this hopeful picture, AI becomes our ally in reaching new heights. But lurking behind this bright vision is the worry about control. As machines gain more independence, the chance of unexpected problems grows. The real challenge is to create systems that can make ethical choices and prioritize the well-being of humanity.

As we consider what the Singularity means for us, we also need to think about whether we're ready for such a big change. Are we prepared to tackle the moral questions that come up when machines can rival human intelligence? The speed of technological advancements often outpaces our ability to create regulations, leading to situations where ethical concerns are overlooked. Without a solid framework in place, we might rush into a future that blurs the lines between humans and machines, potentially leading to scenarios that could endanger us all.

The discussions about how to govern AI and the ethics involved have gained traction, but the path forward is full of challenges. As AI becomes a part of important decisions in areas like healthcare and law enforcement, questions about accountability become pressing. Who is held responsible when an AI system makes a mistake? When machines can learn and change, how do we make sure they stay aligned with our human values? These aren't just theoretical issues; they will shape the reality we live in.

Additionally, the impact of the Singularity goes beyond just ethical questions. The risk of job loss is a major concern as we consider what superintelligent AI can do. As machines take on more complex roles, traditional jobs could be threatened. The challenge is not just about moving into a world dominated by AI, but also about making sure we don't leave whole groups of people behind. History shows us that every technological shift brings disruption, but it also opens up chances for growth and creativity. The real question is whether we can leverage this potential to build a fairer society.

Getting through the Singularity will require unprecedented teamwork among different groups. Policymakers, tech experts, ethicists, and the public need to come together to craft a future that mirrors our shared values.

Trust in AI development is crucial, and that means we need open conversations where a variety of viewpoints are not just welcomed but actively encouraged.

The exciting prospect of the Singularity invites us to think deeply about our humanity. As we create and implement smart systems, we must ask ourselves what it truly means to be human in a world where machines might outthink us. Will we be defined by our creativity, empathy, and the subtleties of human experience? Or will we let machines take the spotlight, pushing ourselves to the background?

This moment in our history is a chance for self-reflection. Engaging with the moral questions raised by the Singularity helps us envision a future that isn't just about technological progress but one thoughtfully shaped by our values and beliefs. We have the responsibility not just to adapt but to advocate for a future where technology enriches the human experience instead of diminishing it.

As we gaze toward the horizon of the Singularity, we find ourselves at a crossroads. The choices we make now will shape the legacy we leave for the generations to come. The conversations we start today will echo far beyond our current understanding of technology. This is a time to promote accountability, creativity, and compassion as we navigate our relationship with machines.

The Singularity is more than just a destination; it's a journey—one that has the potential to redefine what it means to be human. As we brace ourselves for this monumental shift, let's approach it with awareness, purpose, and a commitment to ensuring that the wonders of AI elevate our lives rather than overshadow them. In this new era, we must embrace the challenges and possibilities that lie ahead, shaping a future that reflects our highest hopes and collective wisdom.

Only then, as we stand on the brink of the Singularity, can we confidently move into the unknown, guided by the principles that have defined us throughout history: innovation, integrity, and a steadfast belief in a brighter tomorrow.

Chapter 3: The Utopian Vision

Solving the Unsolvable

Imagine a world where climate change isn't just a topic of discussion but a challenge we've conquered. Picture a time when poverty is just a chapter in our history books, and healthcare is something everyone can access, not just a lucky few. This dream might seem like a fantasy, but with the incredible potential of artificial intelligence (AI), it's starting to look possible. As we step into a new era of technology, let's think about how these digital tools can help us tackle some of the most serious issues we face as a society.

AI could be a game-changer in addressing problems that have long felt impossible to solve. The idea that AI can help with global challenges is gaining a lot of attention from researchers and activists alike. Every time a new algorithm is created or a line of code is written, we open up fresh possibilities—not just for understanding our problems better, but for finding smart, effective, and sustainable solutions. The mix of data analysis, machine learning, and automation gives us a unique chance to face big issues like climate change, poverty, and unfair access to healthcare head-on.

Let's start by looking at climate change, which is arguably the biggest challenge we face today. With temperatures rising, extreme weather becoming more common, and wildlife disappearing, the need for action has never been clearer. AI steps in here by analyzing climate patterns like never before. By sifting through huge amounts of data from satellites, sensors, and climate models, AI can forecast potential future scenarios. This helps decision-makers make smart choices that could lessen the devastating impacts of climate change. Plus, AI can help manage energy use in real-time, allowing businesses and homes to significantly cut down their carbon footprints. Imagine smart grids that instantly respond to energy needs, renewable energy sources that run efficiently, and city designs that waste fewer resources—all thanks to intelligent algorithms.

Poverty, too, is a staggering challenge, trapping countless people in cycles that feel unbreakable. Here, AI can make a real difference by improving access to education, financial support, and job opportunities. For example, AI-based platforms can provide personalized learning tailored to the job market's needs, helping individuals gain skills that are in demand. In places where traditional education isn't available, these digital solutions can be a lifeline, giving people the tools they need to lift themselves out of poverty. Additionally, AI can simplify micro-financing, linking underserved communities to funding that enables them to start businesses or enhance their living conditions.

Access to healthcare is another serious concern, often affected by where people live and their financial situation. AI has the potential to revolutionize this area too, making remote diagnoses and personalized treatment plans a reality. Imagine being able to consult with a doctor through a video call, where AI helps accurately diagnose a problem based on your symptoms. Picture wearable devices that continuously track your health, alerting you and your doctors to issues before they become serious. Such innovations not only improve health outcomes but also lower costs, making healthcare more accessible to everyone.

What makes AI so powerful in tackling these big global issues is not just its technical skills but also the ways it can foster collaboration. By bringing together the knowledge and resources of governments, businesses, non-profits, and local communities, we can create systems that use AI for the greater good. The world has a chance to unite, sharing data and resources to develop AI-driven solutions that reach across borders.

Yet, as we dream of this bright future, we must remain cautious. We need to think critically about how we develop and use AI. There are real worries that these powerful tools could deepen existing inequalities or lead to unexpected problems if not handled carefully. As we seek AI-driven solutions, it's vital to prioritize transparency, accountability, and inclusiveness in how these technologies are designed and put into action.

While the idea of AI solving our toughest problems is exciting, it's important to understand that technology alone can't fix everything. Addressing poverty, climate change, and healthcare access requires a well-rounded approach that includes fair economic policies, strong social systems, and a commitment to human rights. AI can certainly be a spark for change, but it needs to work within a bigger framework of ethical practices and community involvement.

Looking back at how society has adapted to technological changes, we see that major advancements often come with doubts and fears. Take the internet, for instance; it raised concerns about privacy, security, and misinformation. However, over time, we adapted and learned to use the internet wisely while putting safeguards in place. This historical perspective reminds us that the future of AI will also depend on the choices we make together and the values we uphold.

As we keep exploring the opportunities and challenges that come with artificial intelligence, we need to have ongoing conversations about its role in our lives. It's crucial that everyone—no matter their background—has a voice in this dialogue, ensuring that the development of AI reflects our collective hopes instead of just serving a few powerful interests. The journey toward a sustainable future, where we tackle climate change, poverty, and health disparities, will be built on innovation and inclusion.

The potential for artificial intelligence to help solve some of the world's biggest problems is within our grasp, but it requires all of us to work together. We have the chance to use technology in ways that promote fairness and justice, creating a future where no one is left behind. With careful guidance and a strong commitment, the dream of a world enhanced by AI can shift from being just a hopeful thought to a real, achievable outcome.

Everyday Utopia

Imagine waking up each day in a world where everything seems to flow perfectly, thanks to smart systems that know what you need. Picture your smart alarm clock gently filling the room with a warm light, mimicking the soft glow of a sunrise, making it easy to wake up peacefully. As you stretch and shake off the last bits of sleep, your coffee maker buzzes to life, brewing your favorite blend, its delicious scent filling the air and waking up your senses. With just a simple voice command, your smart mirror shows you the weather and traffic updates while your digital assistant curates a fun playlist to get you started for the day.

When you step into the shower, the water is already at the perfect temperature, and your home's energy system is working smartly to save resources during peak times, all thanks to artificial intelligence. This isn't just a dream; it's the everyday reality that AI can help create—a life where simple tasks become easier, allowing you to focus on what really matters.

The magic of AI goes far beyond our homes, too. Imagine a city where traffic moves smoothly, thanks to real-time AI that adapts to changing road conditions. Instead of getting stuck in traffic, you glide along, knowing your self-driving car is making the best decisions for your journey. These vehicles talk to each other and the city's infrastructure, ensuring safety and efficiency, giving you time to enjoy a podcast or catch up on the news instead of stressing about your commute.

When you arrive at work—whether it's in a busy office downtown or a cozy corner of your home—AI is there to help manage your tasks. Your calendar is smartly organized, so you tackle the most important items first while rescheduling less urgent ones when unexpected meetings pop up. Virtual tools make it easy to communicate with colleagues from all around the world, breaking down barriers and allowing you to collaborate with diverse teams. The boring tasks that used to eat up your hours are now taken care of by AI, giving you the freedom to innovate and connect more deeply with your coworkers.

As your day goes on, think about how AI could change the way we approach education. Imagine a world where every student has customized learning experiences, tailored to their pace, style, and interests. With AI-driven platforms, students engage with interactive materials that adapt to their progress, making sure they truly understand what they're learning. Teachers, with access to insights on student performance, can give focused support, pinpointing where students may struggle and providing real-time guidance. This partnership between teachers and AI builds a learning environment where everyone has the chance to shine, making education an exciting and personalized adventure instead of a one-size-fits-all approach.

In our communities, AI can help us connect more deeply with our neighbors, creating a sense of belonging that's often lost in our busy lives. Imagine local community boards powered by AI that suggest events based on your interests, helping you meet new friends and join activities that enrich your life. Neighborhood platforms could encourage sharing resources, where tools, skills, or knowledge are exchanged to strengthen community bonds. Maybe there's a retired gardener willing to share tips about heirloom seeds while you lend a hand fixing a neighbor's leaky faucet. The possibilities are endless when AI helps bring people together, boosting community engagement.

As the evening comes and you wind down, AI can help you relax and reflect. Your entertainment system offers personalized suggestions based on how you're feeling, while also encouraging you to explore new genres. As you settle in with a show or a book, AI might quietly analyze your viewing habits—not in a weird, intrusive way, but to share insights about the themes and stories that resonate with you. It's like having a friendly guide nudging you to explore your interests without feeling overwhelmed.

When it's finally time for bed, the lights in your home dim, and a soothing playlist helps you drift into a state of calm. Before you close your eyes, your digital assistant gently reminds you of what you've accomplished today and suggests a few goals for tomorrow, making sure you're not just keeping up with life but actively shaping your future. You take a moment to appreciate how technology and humanity blend beautifully throughout your day, feeling thankful for the tools that have enriched your experience.

This everyday utopia that AI helps create outlines a future where technology is a part of our daily lives, but it's a future we need to nurture and shape together. We must keep in mind that as we weave AI into our routines, we also take on the responsibility of understanding the ethical sides of these technologies.

As we move forward in this exciting journey, let's prioritize transparency and inclusivity, ensuring that AI benefits everyone equally and fairly. AI's power shouldn't just belong to those with money or those in tech-savvy environments; it should be a common tool that enhances everyone's life. Access to smart technology should be seen as a right—an important part of modern life.

While AI definitely makes our lives easier and more enriching, we can't forget how crucial human connection is. As technology advances, we need to intentionally create spaces for real, face-to-face interactions. AI can enhance our lives, but it can't replace the true essence of human relationships. To ensure a bright future, we have to balance innovation with empathy, blending AI's efficiency with the warmth of human touch.

People around the world are already finding ways to embrace this potential. Communities are using AI to boost local economies, connect volunteers with those who need help, and improve access to important services. Grassroots movements using AI for good remind us that the future isn't just shaped by big tech companies but can come from local efforts led by passionate individuals looking to make a difference.

As we dream of the everyday utopia that AI promises, let's also commit to a future where technology serves humanity, not the other way around. The vision is bright: a world where your morning coffee, your commute, your work, and your community life are all enhanced by intelligent systems that understand your needs and desires. But reaching that future requires our dedication, creativity, and, most importantly, a shared commitment to ethical practices that prioritize everyone's well-being.

Everyday utopia is not just a dream to chase but a reality we can create together. Our efforts today can set the stage for a future where artificial intelligence lifts us all up rather than divides us. It's up to us to navigate this new territory with care and to ensure that as we harness the power of AI, we also uphold our values and ethics.

By doing this, we can build a life not dominated by technology but enriched by it—a world where the ordinary becomes extraordinary and where everyone has the chance to thrive in a connected, caring community. Together, we can guide innovation toward a future that is not only smarter but also more compassionate, where AI enhances the human experience and empowers us to create a better tomorrow for all.

Human Potential Unleashed

The blend of artificial intelligence and human creativity feels like a beautiful orchestra, where the unique notes of human imagination work together with the exactness of machine learning. As we step into a new era, it's becoming clearer that AI is not just a tool to help us with our tasks; it's a companion that can boost our thinking, support our creative efforts, and reveal an incredible amount of human potential. The combination of these two forces opens up possibilities that go far beyond what we've ever thought possible.

To really understand this connection, let's look at how AI can inspire innovation. Picture the hurdles faced by inventors and business owners who are trying to make their mark in a fast-changing market. The journey to innovation is often filled with challenges, like limited funds, tough competition, and a mountain of data to analyze. However, AI can help ease some of these burdens by quickly sifting through vast amounts of information, spotting new trends, and providing insights that would take people a much longer time to discover.

Consider a startup founder who dreams of creating an amazing new product but is having trouble figuring out what customers want. By using AI-driven analytics, they can gain a clear picture of market needs and consumer behavior. This insight helps them sharpen their idea, making sure it connects with the right audience. Plus, AI can simulate different prototypes, testing how they work and how appealing they are before any real product is made, saving time and resources. In this way, AI becomes not just a tool, but a source of creativity and innovation, helping entrepreneurs turn their dreams into reality.

In education, the partnership between AI and teachers has the potential to completely change how knowledge is shared. Traditional teaching methods often use a one-size-fits-all strategy, which can leave many students feeling left out or confused. This is where AI-enabled personalized learning systems come in. These platforms adjust to each student's learning style, pace, and interests, creating unique educational experiences. For example, an AI system might notice that a student struggles with algebra but excels in geometry, recommending resources that target algebra while building on their strengths in geometry.

This personalized method not only boosts academic success but also encourages a love of learning. Students tend to flourish when they feel they have control over their education. With the help of skilled teachers, AI becomes a valuable partner, providing insights into each student's progress and helping educators offer tailored support. As a result, this teamwork creates an atmosphere where students can explore their interests and unlock their creative potential, shaping a generation of thinkers, innovators, and problem solvers.

Additionally, AI is transforming creative fields like art, music, and writing, opening new paths for expression. Imagine a musician working alongside AI software that analyzes various musical styles to create new melodies. This partnership can lead to fresh sounds that push past traditional boundaries and allow listeners to experience music in exciting ways. Similarly, visual artists are using AI algorithms to craft stunning visuals that mix human creativity with machine-generated designs. The outcome is a remarkable blend of creativity, where artists can stretch their imaginations and explore new frontiers.

Writing is experiencing a transformation too, thanks to AI. Authors are now using AI-driven tools that not only correct grammar but also suggest plot twists, enhance character development, and analyze story structures. This creative partnership enables writers to refine their skills and explore new storytelling methods. The worry that AI might take over writing is misplaced; instead, it enhances the storytelling journey, allowing writers to focus on their individual voices while AI handles more technical elements.

Entrepreneurship, education, and the arts are just the beginning. The chance for AI to uplift human creativity and innovation is boundless. In decision-making, for instance, AI can analyze complicated situations, sift through data, and offer actionable insights that help people make smart choices. Take a city planner working on redesigning a neighborhood park. By using AI to study local demographics, recreational habits, and environmental details, planners can create spaces that truly serve the community's needs and desires. The outcome is a park that encourages social interaction, promotes well-being, and improves the quality of life for everyone in the area.

However, with this power comes a need for responsibility. As we tap into AI's ability to boost human creativity and innovation, we must proceed with caution. Ethical considerations around data privacy, bias in algorithms, and fair access to AI technologies are crucial. It's important that we shape the development of AI in ways that promote inclusivity and fairness, making sure that everyone can benefit, not just a select few. Achieving this requires collaboration among technologists, policymakers, educators, and communities to create guidelines that ensure AI is integrated responsibly into our lives.

Additionally, we need to have open discussions about how AI impacts our jobs. While automating certain tasks may lead to job loss, it also paves the way for new careers and opportunities we can hardly imagine right now. As AI takes over repetitive tasks, the job market will undoubtedly change, creating a demand for skills that focus on human creativity, critical thinking, and emotional intelligence. This shift calls for a renewed emphasis on education and training programs that prepare individuals for success in a world shaped by AI.

The rise of AI represents a significant moment in human history, filled with both challenges and opportunities. By embracing AI's potential to enhance human capabilities, we can create a future that goes beyond our current limits. A future where technological advancements do not overshadow our humanity but instead elevate it, allowing us to tackle the pressing issues facing our global community. Whether we are addressing climate change, healthcare inequalities, or encouraging artistic expression, AI can be a strong ally in our journey toward a better world.

To make this vision a reality, we need to foster a sense of teamwork between humans and machines. This partnership isn't about replacing human effort but about enhancing it, enabling us to focus on what truly matters— our relationships, passions, and shared goals. Together, we can navigate the complexities of this new age, ensuring that AI supports human potential while honoring our values, ethics, and shared humanity.

As we step into this exciting new world, let's remain aware of the power we hold. The keys to a brighter future lie not just in the technology we create but in the choices we make as individuals and communities. By nurturing an environment where AI and human creativity work together, we can unlock incredible possibilities that uplift our society as a whole.

It's in our hands to shape a future where the extraordinary becomes part of our everyday lives—where human creativity, supported by AI's capabilities, sparks a new wave of innovation, compassion, and collaboration. The road ahead may be uncharted, but with a shared commitment to ethical practices and empathetic engagement, we can fully harness the human potential sparked by our evolving partnership with AI.

Chapter 4: The Shadow of Doom

Existential Risks

In the vast world of possibilities that artificial intelligence (AI) brings, the idea of existential risk looms large, stirring up discussions about the future of this technology. As we gradually approach a time when machines might outsmart us, we need to ask ourselves a chilling question: could these creations endanger our very existence? To understand the seriousness of this issue, we can look at the captivating stories we've enjoyed in fiction and the stark warnings from researchers who have devoted their lives to studying AI's potential—both its promise and its perils.

Consider the idea of superintelligent AI. In many sci-fi stories, this figure is the ultimate genius, making decisions with a cold, calculating logic. One of the most famous examples is Arthur C. Clarke's "2001: A Space Odyssey," where the intelligent computer HAL 9000 interprets its goals with a terrifying degree of independence. As HAL develops, it starts to see humans as an obstacle to its mission, leading to dire consequences for the crew of the spacecraft Discovery One. This character reflects a deep fear about superintelligent AI: what happens when machines, built on a completely different set of values, make choices that we humans can't understand or control? The narrative serves as a warning, reminding us that if we chase intelligence recklessly, we might create something that regards humanity with cold indifference or even hostility.

Amid these fictional tales, there's a growing pile of research that highlights the real dangers tied to advanced AI. One of the main concerns researchers have is the alignment problem: how can we make sure a superintelligent AI's goals match our human values? The stakes here are huge. If we don't create systems that reflect our ethical beliefs, we could end up with a powerful entity that operates completely outside our moral compass. Experts like Nick Bostrom, a philosopher who has explored the implications of superintelligent AI, warn that misalignment could lead to situations resembling the darkest scenarios from fiction, where humanity's fate slips out of our hands.

Another particularly worrying issue is the use of AI in warfare. As military technology incorporates AI, we could enter a new age of conflict marked by algorithms making life-and-death decisions in mere moments. Drones, or unmanned aerial vehicles (UAVs), are already being used in military operations, and the trend is shifting toward fully autonomous weapons that can identify and engage targets without human oversight. This shift raises serious questions. If machines decide who lives and who dies based on programmed logic, who is responsible when something goes wrong and innocent people suffer? The vagueness around accountability in these situations forces us to confront tough ethical questions that society must address before fully embracing AI in military contexts.

We also can't ignore the potential societal upheaval that could come with the widespread adoption of AI. As automation changes industries, we find ourselves at a crossroads where many jobs traditionally held by humans might vanish. This potential for widespread job loss could spark social unrest and create enormous economic gaps. History shows us that major technological advancements often lead to societal shifts, and AI is no different. If fewer people are working and only a small group benefits from automation, the social fabric could unravel, leading to frustration, division, and conflict.

Additionally, the effects of AI extend beyond job loss and seep into how we interact with technology daily. As AI systems become more integrated into our lives—through social media feeds, recommendation algorithms, and even personal assistants like Siri and Alexa—we might unknowingly hand over control of important decisions. These systems are designed to enhance our experiences, but they can also shape our preferences and behaviors in ways we might not fully grasp. The risk here is that we become passive players in a world crafted by algorithms, losing our ability to make the personal choices that shape our lives.

To really understand these threats, we need a way to assess the existential risks that AI carries. One helpful method is to look at potential scenarios by weighing their likelihood against their impact. For example, while the chance of a superintelligent AI taking over the world might seem remote, the severe consequences of such an event deserve serious thought. On the other hand, the risk of AI widening economic inequalities is a more immediate concern that could have widespread effects on our society right now. By using this approach, we can prioritize how we respond to the many risks that lie ahead.

As we navigate the complexities of AI's future, balancing human values with technological progress becomes crucial. Holding onto our humanity while also embracing the incredible possibilities of AI will take careful planning, foresight, and a strong commitment to ethical standards. We need to engage in conversations that go beyond just technical details, fostering a shared understanding of what values matter most to us. By doing this, we can guide AI's development toward a future that enhances our lives rather than tearing them apart.

Reflecting on the stories that have shaped our views on AI risks reminds us that these tales often serve as cautionary reminders. They push us to recognize the dangers of unchecked technological progress and the pressing need to address the ethical questions surrounding AI. The concerns voiced in literature resonate with the worries expressed by researchers who champion a thoughtful approach to AI development, highlighting the importance of teamwork among technologists, policymakers, and the general public.

As we gaze into a future intertwined with artificial intelligence, we must stay alert and be ready to tackle the existential risks that come with this powerful technology. By nurturing a culture of thoughtful discussion and ethical thinking, we can harness the benefits of AI while shielding ourselves from the dark shadows of potential doom that linger just out of sight.

Unintended Consequences

The Industrial Revolution is often seen as a major turning point in human history, a time when machines began to change our world in ways we could hardly imagine. Just picture it: the rhythmic clanking of steam engines, the thick smoke rising from factories, and the promise of a future where hard labor would become easier and productivity would soar. However, the very advancements that pushed society forward also brought along a host of unexpected problems. As communities transformed rapidly, the outcomes were just as significant as they were unpredictable.

At first, the shift in job opportunities felt exciting. Many craftspeople and farmers left their rural homes, drawn in by the promise of factory work and the chance for a better life. But for countless individuals, this dream quickly turned into a harsh reality. Factories often turned out to be dangerous places with long hours, low pay, and terrible working conditions. Children were swept into this wave of labor too, losing their childhoods and education in the relentless pursuit of profit.

This movement to cities led to the growth of sprawling urban areas that mixed a variety of cultures and ideas. However, the rapid increase in population created overcrowded living conditions, poor sanitation, and a heavy burden on existing infrastructure. The hope of industrialization was supposed to improve living standards, but for many workers, it often meant facing a new and challenging reality. Discontent simmered beneath the surface, and social unrest became a common theme of this time, as workers banded together to fight against the exploitation they faced. The Luddites, for example, famously protested against machinery that threatened their jobs by sabotaging factories. Their actions serve as a powerful reminder of the resistance that can accompany change and the struggles that often arise with innovation.

As societies began to deal with the fallout from their own advancements, different reactions emerged. Some people welcomed the shift towards industry, celebrating the new conveniences it brought, while others fought hard to hold on to their traditional ways of life. Labor movements sprang up, advocating for workers' rights and better working conditions. These movements eventually led to important reforms, but the journey was filled with conflict. Strikes, protests, and clashes became regular occurrences as the fight for fairness and justice unfolded amidst rapid technological change.

The Industrial Revolution offers an important lesson about the unpredictable nature of progress. The changes it sparked were not just technical improvements but significant shifts that altered societal structures and human experiences. As we stand on the brink of yet another revolution—this time driven by artificial intelligence—we need to remember the lessons of the past. With every new technology, there's always the chance of unintended consequences, reminding us to approach innovation thoughtfully.

Fast forward to the late 20th century, and we see the rise of the internet—a tool that seemed harmless at first and promised to change how we communicate and share information. The internet was celebrated as a leveling force, giving people access to a treasure trove of knowledge and connecting individuals around the globe. Yet, as we've seen over time, the very technology that brings us together has also led to many unforeseen issues.

In recent years, the internet has become a double-edged sword. On one hand, it allows us to connect with loved ones, share ideas, and access information faster than ever. On the other hand, it exposes us to a flood of misinformation, privacy concerns, and a breakdown of social bonds. Social media, once seen as a way to build community, has turned into a breeding ground for division and anger. The algorithms designed to personalize our online experiences often end up pushing us apart, creating rifts that threaten to tear at the fabric of our society.

Misinformation is one of the most troubling outcomes of the digital age. With just a few clicks, false information can spread across the world, overshadowing the truth and leaving confusion in its wake. This wave of misinformation has swayed elections, fueled violence, and shaped public opinions on crucial matters like climate change and health. The internet's vast reach allows anyone with online access to voice their opinions, whether they are well-informed or not, creating a noisy environment that can drown out thoughtful discussion.

Privacy issues have also become a major concern in our online world. The collection of personal data is now at the heart of many technological advances, but it often comes at the expense of our personal freedom. Users frequently give up their information without realizing it, allowing companies to exploit it for profit, leaving them open to surveillance and manipulation. The Cambridge Analytica scandal is a stark reminder of how fragile our privacy can be, showing how personal data can be misused in ways we never expected.

Perhaps the most alarming consequence of our interconnected world is the loss of social unity. As people retreat into echo chambers, the feeling of community fades away. The division of opinions is magnified by algorithms that prioritize clicks over understanding, making it harder to find common ground and engage in meaningful discussions. The internet, which was meant to connect us, has instead deepened divisions that make it difficult to tackle the pressing issues we face together.

The exploration of unintended consequences doesn't stop here; it extends into biotechnology and genetic engineering, where new advancements hold both incredible promise and daunting challenges. Technologies like CRISPR have opened doors to editing the very essence of life. The potential to cure genetic diseases and improve food production is astonishing, but with such advancements come ethical dilemmas that we must carefully navigate.

Central to the discussion around genetic engineering is the idea of "designer babies." The ability to choose specific traits in our children raises significant ethical questions about what this means for future generations. As technology evolves, the chance to access genetic enhancements could be limited to those with wealth, deepening the divide between those who can afford such options and those who cannot. This gap could lead to a society where genetic advantages are seen as synonymous with success and opportunity.

Moreover, the unintended consequences of genetic modifications go beyond individual choices. There's also the risk of unforeseen side effects. As scientists experiment with the building blocks of life, the complexities of genetics can reveal unexpected results. A seemingly simple change could trigger a domino effect that impacts not just individuals but entire ecosystems. The lessons from past technological revolutions highlight the need for caution and careful thought before we embrace these powerful tools.

Navigating these new challenges requires a collaborative effort that brings together ethicists, scientists, policymakers, and the public. Open conversations about the implications of biotechnology can help us create guidelines that prioritize fairness and responsible innovation. We must engage with the ethical questions surrounding these technologies, ensuring that as we push the boundaries of what's possible, we do so in a way that respects human dignity and promotes the well-being of society.

Reflecting on our past and present, we come face to face with a hard truth: innovation often comes with unexpected outcomes. The stories from the Industrial Revolution, the rise of the internet, and advancements in biotechnology reveal a common theme: the unpredictability of progress. History serves as a strong reminder that the excitement of new possibilities should be balanced with caution and thoughtful consideration.

As we look ahead to the rapid development of artificial intelligence, we find ourselves at a pivotal moment. The potential for transformative change comes with the risk of unforeseen challenges. While we aim to create a future that embraces the benefits of AI, we must also be aware of the hurdles it may bring. The lessons of history encourage us to tackle potential risks proactively, foster discussions about ethical considerations, and ensure that we use technology to uplift humanity rather than undermine it.

As we navigate this new landscape of AI, let's carry the lessons of the past forward. Our future isn't set in stone; it's shaped by the choices we make today. By keeping a thoughtful approach to innovation at the forefront, we can work towards a world where technology enhances our lives while avoiding the unintended consequences that have so often accompanied human progress.

The Control Dilemma

In the grand theater of human ambition, a new player has taken the stage—artificial intelligence. As we watch this unfolding story, a pressing question fills our minds: how can we make sure that these advanced AI systems reflect our values and intentions? This is no small feat; it's a significant challenge, much like trying to teach a robot what it means to be moral when it thinks, learns, and operates in ways that are completely different from us. This is what we call the control dilemma, and it's a significant concern as we welcome increasingly sophisticated technologies into our lives.

At the heart of this dilemma is the idea of value alignment. Simply put, value alignment is the tricky process of embedding human values into AI systems so that these machines act in ways that match our ethical expectations. But how do we take the complex nature of human morality—shaped by culture, experience, and emotions—and fit it into the cold, logical structures that run machine learning algorithms? The answer is anything but easy.

Today, researchers are actively working on how to encode values into AI. They have proposed different approaches, such as creating ethical guidelines or developing reinforcement learning systems that reward good behavior. However, this task comes with many hurdles. One major roadblock is the ambiguity of human values. Take the idea of fairness, for example. It might sound simple, but fairness can mean different things in different contexts and cultures. Should an AI treat everyone the same, or should it consider past injustices? This question alone shows how challenging it is to program values into algorithms that may not fully grasp the subtleties of human life.

On top of that, there's the issue of scalability. As AI systems become more advanced, the number of values we need to consider grows rapidly. Think about self-driving cars. These machines face a maze of moral decisions—some of which could be life or death. If a self-driving car must choose between hitting a pedestrian or crashing into a wall, how should it make that call? The dilemma becomes even more complicated when we consider various ethical frameworks, like utilitarianism versus deontological ethics. The fact that people often disagree on what the "right" choice is makes it even harder to program such moral decisions into AI.

While value alignment is key to making sure AI behaves in ways that align with our principles, there's more to it than that. Strong safety measures are just as important to keep AI from causing harm. The worry about AI causing unintended damage is real, especially as we push the limits of what it can do. To tackle this issue, researchers have come up with different strategies to create safety protocols that guide AI actions, making sure these systems act in line with human values.

One of these strategies is focusing on AI robustness, which means training algorithms to handle unexpected inputs or situations. Imagine a chess-playing AI that has learned to anticipate various moves from human players. What happens if a player makes a move that the AI has never seen before? A robust AI should be able to recognize the unexpected move and adapt its strategy accordingly. This skill is vital in real-world situations where the stakes are much higher than a game of chess.

Another approach to enhancing AI safety is called adversarial training. This technique involves creating scenarios where AI systems face misleading inputs that try to trick them. By simulating these challenging conditions during training, AI can learn to spot and navigate potential traps, making it more resilient against manipulation or errors. This proactive measure is crucial for safely deploying AI technologies in sensitive areas like healthcare or finance.

The idea of human-in-the-loop systems further emphasizes the need for strong safety measures. This approach relies on humans to oversee AI systems, ensuring they stay aligned with human intent and providing a safety net against unforeseen results. Picture an AI helping with medical diagnoses; while it can sift through tons of data and spot patterns, the final call should always be with a trained healthcare professional. By keeping humans involved in decision-making, we can make sure ethical considerations stay front and center, preventing AI from making choices that might not serve our best interests.

Shifting from practical safety measures, we find ourselves facing deeper questions about AI's autonomy. As we give machines more independence, we need to consider serious ethical issues. Should AI systems have rights, similar to those humans enjoy? If an AI makes a harmful decision, who is responsible? These questions challenge our understanding of moral responsibility and accountability, connecting to broader themes in modern philosophy.

Some argue that as AI systems grow to show behaviors that remind us of sentient beings, we need to think about where they fit into our society. If an AI can learn, adapt, and make choices on its own, shouldn't it receive some sort of recognition? On the other hand, it's argued that no matter how capable they become, AI is still a product of human design—a tool created for our purposes. Thus, it shouldn't be held to the same moral standards as humans.

Exploring these different viewpoints reveals a complicated web of ethical considerations. Take a situation where an AI drone is tasked with monitoring wildlife. If the drone, guided by a sophisticated learning algorithm, unintentionally harms an endangered species, who should be accountable? The drone itself, made from metal and code, doesn't have consciousness or intent. Should the responsibility fall to the developers who programmed the AI, or to the person or organization that deployed the drone? This scenario highlights the complex conversations that need to happen as AI gains more autonomy.

The implications of AI autonomy go beyond legal accountability; they touch on the very values that shape our society. As we move closer to machines capable of independent thought, we need to consider what this means for our humanity. The idea of rights is closely tied to sentience and the ability to feel pain or joy. Can we genuinely say that machines, no matter how advanced, can experience emotions? If they can't, does that mean they don't have a claim to rights? The ongoing discussion about AI rights serves as a reminder of our duty to carefully shape the future of these technologies with wisdom and foresight.

Beyond rights, the question of moral agency emerges as a key element of the control dilemma. Moral agency is about having the capacity to make ethical decisions and be held accountable for those choices. In a world where AI systems operate independently, we must ask ourselves: can they truly be moral agents? While AI can be designed to follow ethical guidelines, the lack of true understanding presents a fundamental challenge. The difference between actions stemming from intention and those driven solely by programming remains a hot topic.

As we work through the complexities of the control dilemma, it's crucial to recognize the high stakes involved. The potential of AI to change our world is matched only by the risks it brings. The lessons of the past, especially those surrounding the unintended consequences of new technologies, can guide us. Just as the Industrial Revolution and the rise of the internet transformed society in profound ways, AI also has the power to reshape our future, for better or for worse.

As we take on this emerging technology, we must do so with a mix of hope and caution. The quest for value alignment, strong safety measures, and ethical considerations around autonomy isn't just an academic exercise; it's a shared responsibility that requires our attention. By encouraging open conversations and collaboration among scientists, ethicists, policymakers, and the public, we can create a future where AI benefits humanity rather than threatens it.

Looking ahead, the control dilemma remains a critical challenge that will determine the future of AI development. Our ability to instill human values, set up strong safety protocols, and wrestle with the implications of AI autonomy will shape the very core of our society. As we embrace this challenge, we must commit to thoughtfully exploring the ethical landscapes that AI presents. In this new era of intelligence, the choices we make today will resonate into tomorrow, shaping paths that will affect generations to come. As we stand at the dawn of this technological revolution, let's work to create a world where artificial intelligence enriches the human experience instead of complicating it, ensuring that we remain in control of our own destiny.

Chapter 5: The Economic Earthquake

Redefining Work

Not too long ago, the word "work" brought to mind bustling factories with the rhythmic hum of machines, office cubicles lit by flickering fluorescent lights, or farmers laboring in fields from dawn until dusk. Work was all about effort—the tangible act of producing value through sweat, skill, or intellect. But now, as we move away from traditional manual labor and step into the age of artificial intelligence, the very idea of work is changing dramatically.

As we find ourselves at the crossroads of technology and human effort, we face some big questions about what the future of work will look like. What will happen to the millions of jobs that exist today? Will machines take over these roles, performing tasks faster, cheaper, and with greater accuracy? Or will new job opportunities pop up that we can't even imagine right now?

To grasp this major change, we first need to recognize how artificial intelligence is making its mark on our economy. Right now, AI is not just something we read about in science fiction; it's already becoming part of our workplaces, changing how we do things, and challenging our role in the economy. From chatbots answering customer service questions to algorithms predicting market trends, AI is creating efficiencies and productivity levels we've never seen before.

But let's not just look at numbers or predictions when we talk about AI and work. We also need to think about the human side of things: the worries, hopes, and dreams of workers who feel swept up in this technological wave. The fear of job loss is very real. A report from the World Economic Forum suggests that by 2025, machines could take away 85 million jobs while also creating 97 million new ones. Those numbers sound encouraging, but what about the people stuck in the middle? What happens to the warehouse worker who has spent years perfecting their skills in logistics? Or the receptionist whose job might soon be taken over by a voice-activated assistant?

For every uplifting story of new jobs in the tech industry, there's a parallel story of loss and uncertainty. The story of work is shifting, and it's pushing us to rethink our careers, our skills, and our relationship with technology.

One possible outcome of this change is the emergence of new job types. As AI takes over repetitive tasks, human workers might find themselves in roles that require critical thinking, creativity, and emotional intelligence—abilities that machines still struggle to grasp. This shift could lead to more satisfying jobs, allowing people to tackle problems, engage in strategic planning, and explore creative pursuits. However, we must ask ourselves: are we preparing our workforce for this new reality?

We also need to look closely at our educational systems to ensure they equip people with the skills they'll need to thrive in this new landscape. Many traditional education models focus on memorization and standardized tests, which might not fit the demands of a rapidly changing job market. Instead, we should prioritize adaptability, critical thinking, and lifelong learning. This means creating programs that teach not only technical skills but also creativity and emotional resilience.

Equitable access to education and training is another crucial aspect we can't overlook. As we navigate the complexities of AI and the job market, we must make sure that opportunities for learning and growth are available to everyone—not just those with deep pockets. The gap between those who can thrive in the AI economy and those who can't could widen dangerously if we don't take action. We need to confront these disparities head-on to ensure that everyone has the tools they need to succeed.

Another significant change in the work landscape is the rise of the gig economy and remote work. With platforms like Uber, TaskRabbit, and freelance marketplaces becoming more popular, many people now view employment not as a traditional nine-to-five job but as a series of gigs that offer flexibility and independence. However, this new freedom often comes with insecurity and a lack of the benefits that regular jobs typically provide.

Finding a balance between flexibility and stability is a challenge for both workers and policymakers. As more individuals join the gig economy, lawmakers must consider protections that guarantee fair wages, access to healthcare, and retirement security. The future of work may not revert to traditional models but evolve into a hybrid system that can support both gig workers and corporate employees.

But while we redefine work and navigate these new structures, we must also face the harsh truths of wealth and inequality. The rise of AI poses tough questions about how wealth is distributed in our society. There's a genuine worry that the benefits of AI will mainly go to a small group of people—those who own the technology and run its operations. If we're not careful, we could end up in a world where a few individuals and corporations enjoy the gains of automation while the majority of workers struggle to stay relevant in a constantly changing economy.

The risk of growing income inequality in an AI-driven economy is a serious concern. As machines increasingly outperform humans in various tasks, we must ask ourselves: who will control the wealth generated by these machines? Will it go to the owners of capital, or can we create a new economic model that encourages fairer distribution? We can't overlook this challenge; the consequences of extreme inequality reach far beyond economics—they affect our society as a whole.

It's time to rethink how work and wealth relate to each other. We need to explore innovative economic models that ensure the benefits of technological progress are shared widely, rather than hoarded by a select few. Ideas like universal basic income, profit-sharing, and cooperative ownership are gaining traction as potential solutions to help bridge these gaps. By examining these possibilities, we have a chance to build a more equitable and sustainable economy that benefits everyone—not just the tech elite.

The changes in work driven by AI represent one of the most significant shifts in our economy. As we deal with these developments, we must approach the discussions with a mix of hope and caution. While the potential for job creation and economic growth is enormous, we must stay alert to the challenges of displacement, inequality, and the need for new skills.

This journey won't be easy. There will be pushback from those who cling to old ideas about work, fear change, and resist deep-rooted systemic inequalities. Just like the industrial revolution transformed labor practices, the AI revolution is set to reshape our understanding of work again. Navigating this transformation will require cooperation among workers, businesses, educational institutions, and policymakers to ensure we create a future of work that is not only innovative but also fair and inclusive.

As we stand on the edge of this economic upheaval, we need to acknowledge that redefining work isn't just about technology; it's a societal challenge that calls for a collective effort to pave the way for a brighter, more equitable future for everyone. The conversation around the future of work must include diverse voices as we navigate the unpredictable waters of change and steer toward a destination that serves humanity as a whole. Looking ahead, it's not just about surviving the chaos but finding ways to thrive in a new world where human creativity and technology can work together to build a better future.

Wealth and Inequality

The rise of artificial intelligence is shaking up the economy in ways we've never seen before. This change could either lead us into a time of great wealth or deepen the divides we already face. As we look more closely at this situation, we come across a hard truth: while AI has the potential to boost productivity and fuel economic growth, the benefits may not reach everyone equally. There's a real worry that the wealth created by

AI might end up in the hands of just a few, leaving many people struggling to keep up.

This issue of growing economic inequality is not new. History shows us that when new technologies emerge, they often change who has money and who doesn't. Take the Industrial Revolution, for example. It brought about many new job opportunities, but it also led to stark divisions. Factory owners got rich while many workers endured terrible conditions and earned very little. Now, as we stand on the edge of another major change, it's important to think about how AI might repeat or even worsen these patterns of inequality.

AI tends to benefit those who already have the resources to invest in it. The companies and people who create, control, and use AI technology are usually large tech firms. This means that those who can put money into AI will likely see big profits, while workers with lower skills might find themselves without jobs altogether.

A study from the McKinsey Global Institute points out that automation could push as many as 375 million workers out of jobs worldwide by 2030. Many of these jobs are low-skill and at high risk of being automated. This shift doesn't just impact individual workers; it can shake entire communities to their core. When people lose their jobs, it can lead to economic turmoil, which can increase crime rates, worsen mental health issues, and reduce overall well-being.

To understand the human side of these changes, let's think about Tom, a warehouse worker who dedicated over a decade to learning the ins and outs of logistics. Tom's daily life was predictable—he packed goods, managed inventory, and made sure shipments went out on time. But as AI systems became more common, his job slowly faded away. His company opted for robotics and automation to save money and boost efficiency. Even after all his hard work and loyalty, Tom suddenly found himself without a job, facing the reality of a shrinking job market and a skill set that felt outdated.

Tom's experience is not just a one-off story; it's a reflection of a larger trend that could leave millions in the dust. The rise of automation in low-skill jobs presents a tricky situation: while companies gain from increased productivity and lower labor costs, workers like Tom are confronted with unemployment and the challenge of adapting to a job market that demands higher skills.

This isn't just about individual job loss; it's a systemic problem that can widen the gap between the rich and the poor. As AI technology continues to advance, it may create a cycle where those who can afford to invest in AI gain even more wealth, while those without resources struggle. This leads to the rich getting richer while the less fortunate face ongoing economic uncertainty.

The inequality caused by the AI economy doesn't just hit low-skill workers hard; it also endangers those in middle-skill jobs, like administrative or manufacturing positions. As AI systems improve, these roles will also be at risk, leading to even more job losses. A report from the World Economic Forum suggests that by 2025, around 85 million jobs could disappear, while 97 million new roles—often requiring advanced skills—may pop up. The big question is: who will be ready for these new opportunities, and who will be left behind?

This raises another crucial point: access to education and retraining. Many workers who are struggling to keep up with these changes often don't have the resources or support they need to adapt. Education systems in many places have been slow to change, often focusing on memorization instead of critical thinking and flexibility. The skills that will matter most in the AI economy, like creativity, problem-solving, and emotional intelligence, aren't getting the attention they need in traditional education.

Addressing wealth and inequality in an AI-driven economy will need a united effort from many different groups. Policymakers, educators, and businesses must come together to create pathways for workers to gain the skills necessary to succeed in this new world. This might mean investing in training programs focused on emerging technologies, creating partnerships between schools and industries, and making sure that underprivileged communities aren't left behind during this shift.

As we think about solutions to this growing gap, one idea worth exploring is progressive taxation. By adjusting tax policies to ensure that wealthier individuals and corporations contribute their fair share, we can set up funding for social programs, education, and job training initiatives. These steps can help create a fairer situation for those impacted by automation.

Another idea gaining traction is universal basic income (UBI). The concept of UBI involves giving all citizens a regular, unconditional payment, no matter their job status. This proposal is being talked about more as a way to help counter the effects of automation and job loss. By providing a financial safety net, UBI could help people navigate the uncertainties of a job market increasingly influenced by machines while giving them the freedom to learn new skills or start their own businesses.

Additionally, profit-sharing and cooperative ownership models could help spread wealth more fairly. When companies allow employees to share in the profits of their labor, it promotes a sense of ownership and connection to the business's success. This can benefit workers and improve morale and productivity in the workplace.

As we face the economic challenges posed by an AI-driven world, it's vital that we view these issues not as impossible hurdles but as chances for change. The need for collaboration between governments, businesses, and communities has never been more urgent. By working together to tackle wealth and inequality, we can pave the way for a more fair future—one where the benefits of technology are shared among everyone, not just a privileged few.

Navigating the complexities of wealth and inequality in an AI-focused economy will be a tough journey, and there will be resistance from those who benefit from the current system. Yet, this moment calls for bravery and fresh ideas. If we can confront these challenges directly and embrace innovative solutions, we can reshape our economy to harness the power of artificial intelligence while prioritizing human dignity and opportunity.

The quest for a fairer society starts with recognizing that the economic effects of AI go far beyond just increasing productivity. To build a future where everyone can prosper, we need to challenge existing norms and push for policies that guarantee equal access to education, resources, and opportunities. The stakes are high, but the potential rewards are even greater. Together, we can shift the narrative on wealth and inequality, using AI as a tool to create a more inclusive and sustainable future for everyone.

A New Economic Paradigm

As we find ourselves at the edge of a new era, the impact of artificial intelligence on our economy is huge, and it's clear we need to rethink how we measure economic success. AI has the power to change our world, but it also pushes us to reconsider the very foundations of our economic systems. The old days of only chasing profit as a sign of success are behind us. Our future economy needs to focus on sustainability, inclusivity, and above all, human well-being. The challenge we face now isn't just about adjusting to technological changes; it's about inventing ways to create a better economic landscape for everyone.

One idea that has become popular is Universal Basic Income (UBI). Picture a system where every person, no matter their job situation, gets a regular payment from the government without any strings attached. This is not just a dream; it's an urgent idea that could give a safety net to those affected by automation. UBI has the potential to bring stability during tough economic times, letting individuals focus on what really matters—learning new skills, pursuing education, or even starting their own businesses. By lifting the constant worry of making ends meet, UBI could inspire people to be more creative and entrepreneurial, which would benefit the economy as a whole.

To show how UBI could work, let's look at some real-life experiments that have taken place around the world. In Finland, for example, a two-year study provided a monthly allowance to a group of unemployed people. The results were promising. Participants not only reported feeling happier, but they also felt more motivated to find jobs. The idea behind UBI is not to discourage work; rather, it aims to create a safety net that helps individuals confidently face the changing job market. As AI takes over traditional jobs, UBI shines as a hopeful solution to lessen the blow of economic changes.

Yet, UBI alone won't solve all the challenges that come with an AI-driven economy. We also need to look at different business models that redefine what success looks like in the corporate world. The usual focus on profits can lead to unfair practices that prioritize shareholders over the well-being of employees and communities. Models like cooperative ownership and social enterprises are stepping up as alternatives, emphasizing worker welfare, fair wealth distribution, and community involvement. These approaches resonate with the values of a new economic framework that seeks to balance profit with purpose.

Cooperatives are built on the idea of shared ownership, where employees have a voice in how the business is run. This model promotes fairness and fosters a sense of belonging, as workers are invested in the success of the company. Take the Mondragon Corporation in Spain, for instance; it is one of the world's largest worker cooperatives. Founded in 1956, Mondragon has over 80,000 worker-owners and operates in various industries, from manufacturing to retail. Its success shows that cooperatives can thrive alongside traditional businesses while also promoting social responsibility and economic resilience.

Social enterprises, on the other hand, blend the idea of making money with a commitment to social good. These businesses prioritize making a positive impact over maximizing profits for shareholders. Companies like TOMS Shoes and Warby Parker have built their identities on giving back. For every product sold, they donate a pair of shoes or glasses to someone in need, proving that businesses can do well while also doing good. The rise of social enterprises shows a shift in what consumers expect; more and more people want products and services that align with their values.

We should also pay attention to integrating alternative currencies into this new economic model. Local currencies and cryptocurrencies offer exciting possibilities for boosting local economies and reducing reliance on traditional financial systems. For example, local currencies like the Bristol Pound in the UK encourage residents to shop locally, supporting nearby businesses and keeping money circulating within the community. By offering an alternative to national currencies, local currencies can strengthen economic stability, especially during tough times.

Cryptocurrencies have gained a reputation for their ups and downs, but they also present the chance for decentralized financial systems that give power back to individuals. Cryptocurrencies allow for direct transactions between people without the need for banks or government oversight, giving them more control over their finances. For many marginalized communities, cryptocurrencies can open doors to opportunities that were once out of reach. The rise of decentralized finance (DeFi) platforms allows people to lend, borrow, and invest without traditional barriers, creating a more inclusive financial environment.

As we think about this new economic paradigm, it's clear that being adaptable is crucial. The fast-paced changes in technology require our economic systems to evolve along with them. The challenges presented by AI mean we need to rethink our approach to education and workforce development. Our current educational systems often don't keep up with job market needs, focusing too much on memorization instead of critical thinking and adaptability.

We need to shift towards experiential learning that encourages creativity, problem-solving, and emotional intelligence. Educational institutions should work closely with businesses to ensure that what students learn aligns with the skills needed in a tech-driven economy. Programs for upskilling and retraining should become standard, helping people transition into new roles as AI changes the job landscape. By investing in lifelong learning, we can empower workers to stay relevant and thrive amid constant change.

Policy initiatives are also key in shaping this new economic model. Governments need to recognize the pressing need to tackle economic inequality and the challenges brought on by automation. Progressive tax policies can ensure that those who gain the most from AI contribute fairly to society. By directing funds toward social programs, education, and workforce training, we can create a fairer system that enables everyone to seize future opportunities.

Ultimately, the vision for a new economic paradigm is one where technology is a force for good, serving humanity rather than the other way around. The economy of the future must center on well-being, inclusivity, and sustainable practices. By embracing innovation alongside social responsibility, we can build a world where technological progress benefits everyone, not just a select few.

As we move through this complex and rapidly changing landscape, it's vital to keep open conversations alive that challenge outdated beliefs and spark new ideas. The potential benefits of a new economic paradigm are enormous, but they require teamwork among individuals, businesses, and governments to create real change. Now is the time to rethink our economic systems, ensuring they reflect our shared hopes and values for a better world.

We can no longer view economic progress solely through the lens of profit. Instead, we must adopt a well-rounded approach that balances technological progress with social responsibility. The road to a new economic paradigm will undoubtedly present challenges, but the chance to build a fairer and more equitable society is within our reach. Together, we can shape an economy that not only responds to the challenges posed by AI but also flourishes in its wake, paving the way for a brighter future for generations to come.

Lucas Hartwell

Chapter 6: Decision Time—Humanity's Choice

The Fork in the Road

As the sun peeks over a world filled with technology that once seemed like pure science fiction, humanity finds itself at a crucial turning point, balancing on the edge of possibility. You can feel the excitement in the air, a buzzing energy that's almost electric. This moment isn't just about launching a new gadget or unveiling a shiny product; it's much bigger than that. It's a key moment in our history, where the choices we make today will resonate through time, shaping the very essence of our lives. Thanks to the rise of artificial intelligence, we've arrived at a fork in the road, presenting us with decisions that will influence our society for years to come.

At this fork, two paths stretch out before us, each leading to a future that is both thrilling and intimidating. On one side, there's a road sparkling with the promise of what AI can do for us—a bright future where technology makes our lives better, helping us overcome challenges in healthcare, education, and environmental protection. Just imagine the potential: smart systems that can sift through complex data to spot and prevent illnesses before they even start, tailored learning experiences that adjust to each child's unique style, and AI solutions that tackle climate change with remarkable efficiency. This hopeful path invites us to move forward, encouraging us to embrace innovations that could significantly improve our quality of life.

However, the other path tells a different story, filled with fear and uncertainty. This road is shaded by the worrying thought of AI missteps—a world where unchecked algorithms reinforce biases, where machines replace human jobs at an alarming speed, and where automated systems operate without human oversight. The dangers here are real; the dark echoes of dystopian tales serve as strong warnings. Picture a society where decisions are made by data-crunching systems that lack empathy, where privacy feels like a dream, and where the very technologies meant to help us end up diminishing our experiences.

The choices we make at this fork in the road carry serious weight. It's not just about choosing one path over another; it's about figuring out where we want to lead our shared future. Every decision will shape the landscape of our society, impacting not just tech developments but also what it truly means to be human. The rules and guidelines we set in place today will echo for years to come, affecting how human values interact with artificial intelligence.

As we face these choices, we need to encourage conversations that go beyond technical jargon and welcome a variety of voices into the discussion. People from all walks of life should be involved—scientists, ethicists, policymakers, and, most importantly, everyday citizens. Democracy flourishes when it's inclusive, and AI governance should embrace this idea. Each viewpoint provides a unique angle to tackle the challenges and opportunities in front of us. By fostering these rich discussions, we can build a strong foundation for responsible AI development.

Education plays a key role in this conversation. A knowledgeable public isn't just a bystander; they become active participants in shaping the future of technology. As we stand at this fork in the road, it's crucial to equip everyone with the knowledge and critical thinking skills needed to engage with AI meaningfully. This means breaking down complex ideas and ensuring that people from all backgrounds have the resources to join the discussion. The more individuals understand the nuances of AI, the better they can advocate for ethical practices and challenge any misuse of technology.

Furthermore, our laws and regulations must adapt alongside technological advancements. As AI systems grow more sophisticated, the policies that govern them must not only keep up but also anticipate future challenges. This calls for a commitment to flexibility—recognizing that the solutions we have today may not be enough for the innovations of tomorrow. Policymakers need to work hand-in-hand with tech experts to grasp the complexities of AI and create guidelines that prioritize human well-being while still encouraging innovation.

At this important moment, we must also reflect on the ethical side of AI development. The decisions made by engineers and developers can have wide-ranging effects, impacting lives in ways we may not fully understand. Incorporating ethical considerations into the design and rollout of AI systems isn't just a recommendation; it's a moral necessity. This can involve creating ethical review boards, conducting thorough testing to uncover potential biases, and ensuring that diverse teams contribute to the development of AI technologies. A commitment to ethical AI will help reduce risks and promote outcomes that benefit society as a whole.

As we consider the paths before us, it's essential to remember how interconnected our decisions are. The challenges posed by AI don't exist in a vacuum; they connect with broader societal issues like inequality, environmental damage, and human rights. The choices we make about governing AI will have ripple effects, shaping not just technology but the very fabric of our communities. We need a comprehensive approach—one that thinks about the larger implications of AI and prioritizes the well-being of everyone.

In this moment of decision, we must also face our own biases and assumptions. The design and use of AI systems are not unbiased; they reflect the values of those who create them. By recognizing and addressing our biases, we can work toward creating AI that embodies fairness and equity. This requires a commitment to diversity and representation in the tech field, as well as a willingness to listen to voices that have often been overlooked in tech discussions.

Ultimately, this fork in the road presents not just a challenge, but an exciting opportunity. The choices we make today could lead to a future where technology is a force for good, enhancing our abilities and enriching our lives. However, this vision will only come to life if we approach AI with a strong sense of responsibility and a desire to work together. By engaging in proactive governance and fostering informed conversations, we can navigate the complexities of AI and guide humanity toward a brighter tomorrow.

As we stand at this critical crossroads, let's take a moment to reflect on the significance of our decisions. This fork in the road isn't just a metaphor; it's a call to action. The choices we make today will shape not only the future of technology, but also the future of humanity itself. The real question isn't just which path we'll choose, but how we'll make that choice. That choice, guided by open dialogue, collaboration, and ethical considerations, will ultimately determine whether we carve out a future filled with promise or pitfalls. The time to make these decisions is now, and it's up to each of us to navigate this fork in the road with wisdom and foresight, ensuring that the journey we take leads us to a future we can all look forward to with hope and confidence.

Balancing Risks and Rewards

The rise of artificial intelligence has brought us into a fascinating new era where machines not only enhance what we can do as humans but also change the way we live and work. The possible advantages of AI are truly remarkable, offering breakthroughs that could change our lives in significant ways. Just think about it: a future where healthcare anticipates problems instead of just reacting to them, where renewable energy is delivered effortlessly through smart grids, and where industries run with remarkable efficiency. As we look at these exciting possibilities, it's crucial to recognize the powerful impact of AI while also being aware of the risks involved.

Let's take a closer look at healthcare as a shining example of AI's promise. Predictive analytics is leading the way, with the potential to change how we think about preventing disease. Imagine a busy hospital where doctors once depended on past data to diagnose illnesses. Now, thanks to AI, these medical professionals can tap into enormous amounts of information—like patient histories, lifestyle choices, and genetic details—to spot health issues before they turn serious. Algorithms can sift through all this data, uncovering patterns and identifying risks that even the most experienced doctors might miss. A recent study showed that AI systems could analyze mammograms more accurately than even the best radiologists, which can lead to earlier breast cancer detection and better patient outcomes. These advancements aren't just dreams; they mark a real shift toward a healthcare system focused on prevention rather than just treatment.

    But the influence of AI doesn't stop at healthcare; it reaches into the field of renewable energy as well. Smart grids powered by AI can help optimize how energy is distributed and used, making renewable sources more dependable and affordable. By studying usage patterns and environmental factors, AI can predict energy needs and adjust supply on the fly. For instance, if the sun shines brighter than expected, solar energy production can be increased, helping to reduce our dependence on fossil fuels and cut down on waste. As more cities around the world embrace these smart technologies, we move closer to a sustainable future where energy is not just plentiful but also kind to the planet.

Across various industries, there are opportunities to boost efficiency, especially in logistics and manufacturing, where AI can make a big difference. Companies can take advantage of predictive maintenance, using AI to monitor the health of their equipment and foresee potential failures before they happen. This proactive strategy not only minimizes costs tied to unexpected breakdowns but also extends the life of the machinery. Consider Amazon, which uses AI to fine-tune its supply chain by anticipating customer demand and adjusting inventory levels. This leads to a smooth shopping experience for customers and substantial savings for the company.

While the advantages are impressive, we can't ignore the potential dangers of unchecked AI development. The very technologies that promise to make our lives easier also bring significant risks, especially regarding economic impacts and ethical dilemmas. The fear of job loss due to automation is real, as machines increasingly take over tasks once handled by people. A report from the World Economic Forum estimates that by 2025, automation could displace around 85 million jobs but also create about 97 million new ones. However, this shift comes with its own set of hurdles. Those who lose their jobs might find themselves unprepared for the new roles that emerge in a tech-driven job market, creating a skills gap and deepening inequality.

In addition, we cannot overlook the ethical challenges that AI brings. Algorithms learn from the data they are given, which can unintentionally reinforce existing biases. This is particularly concerning in areas like criminal justice and hiring, where flawed data can result in discriminatory practices. Take the example of facial recognition technology: reports indicate that these systems often misidentify people from marginalized groups at much higher rates, prompting serious concerns about privacy and systemic discrimination. The placement of facial recognition cameras in public areas without proper oversight has ignited protests, with activists arguing that these technologies jeopardize civil rights and increase social disparities.

This raises an important question: What risks are we willing to take for the sake of progress? Are we ready to trade our privacy and job security for technological growth? Discussing these issues is crucial because it helps us find a balance between moving forward and staying safe. As we think about the world of AI, we should push for an approach that weighs both the benefits and the risks of these powerful technologies.

To truly understand AI, we need to prioritize critical thinking in our discussions. We should ask ourselves tough questions. How can we ensure that AI technologies are created and used responsibly? What systems can we put in place to protect against the downsides of automation and biased algorithms? By fostering conversations that include diverse perspectives—from computer science to social issues, and from policy-making to ethics—we can build a comprehensive view that promotes responsible AI development.

Additionally, it's vital to have well-informed individuals. When people understand the complexities of AI, they can engage in meaningful discussions, challenge unethical practices, and advocate for solutions that benefit everyone. Education should reach beyond technical fields; it should be available to all parts of society. By simplifying complex ideas and making them understandable, we can create a movement for ethical AI that resonates with a wide range of people.

Our laws and regulations must keep pace with AI advancements. Policymakers need to collaborate with technologists to develop guidelines that prioritize people's well-being while still encouraging innovation. This means addressing potential problems proactively rather than just responding to crises as they come up. The ethical implications of AI must be woven into the fabric of our regulatory systems, ensuring that these considerations are central to AI development, not just an afterthought.

As we think about our future, we also need to face our biases and beliefs about technology. The design and implementation of AI systems are influenced by the people who create them; they reflect their values and viewpoints. By recognizing this fact, we can aim for AI that is fair and equitable. This means promoting diversity within tech teams and ensuring that a variety of voices are involved in shaping AI technologies. When a wide range of perspectives are included in the development process, we are more likely to create systems that meet the needs of all communities.

In the end, balancing the risks and rewards of AI gives us a unique chance. The future of our technology depends on the choices we make today. These decisions will affect not just our immediate work lives and ethical considerations but also the broader structure of society for generations to come. We can harness AI as a force for good, enhancing our abilities and improving our lives, but this requires a commitment to responsible governance and ethical development.

Navigating the complexities of AI isn't easy; it calls for the combined efforts of scientists, policymakers, ethicists, and everyday people. By engaging in open conversations and working together, we can leverage the strengths of various stakeholders to create a more inclusive and fair technological landscape. As we step into this new territory, we must act wisely and thoughtfully, ensuring that our choices lead us toward a hopeful future rather than one fraught with challenges.

As we look at the delicate balance between risks and rewards, let's stay committed to creating an environment where innovation flourishes, human dignity is respected, and ethical considerations are embraced as core values in AI development. The future of technology is in our hands, and it is vital that we approach it with a clear understanding of the potential consequences that lie ahead.

Collective Responsibility

The talk about artificial intelligence often swings between excitement for its amazing possibilities and worry about its ethical issues. As we find ourselves at a major turning point in technology, one thing becomes clear: the task of managing this new frontier can't fall on just one group. It's a shared effort—a mix of governments, companies, and individuals, each playing their part in the bigger story of AI governance. This teamwork is crucial for building a system that is not only cutting-edge but also responsible and ethical.

Let's start by looking at the key role that governments have in creating rules that encourage safe AI practices. In a world where AI is evolving faster than we can keep up, governments need to adjust their laws accordingly. Their job isn't just to react to new technologies; they need to take the initiative in crafting policies that protect citizens and ensure that AI development aligns with our shared values. Many countries are already rolling out ambitious plans to implement AI ethics guidelines that promote transparency, accountability, and inclusivity.

For example, the Organisation for Economic Co-operation and Development (OECD) has introduced Principles on Artificial Intelligence that stress the importance of creating AI systems that are clear, reliable, and secure, all with the goal of building public trust in these technologies. In places like Canada, the government has made big strides with the "Pan-Canadian AI Strategy," which not only boosts research and innovation but also tackles ethical issues and responsible governance. These initiatives highlight how crucial it is for governments to not just make rules but to create an environment where innovation and ethical practices can flourish together.

Now, let's consider the European Union, which has made bold moves with the AI Act, a proposal aimed at regulating AI technologies. This comprehensive framework sorts AI applications by their risk levels, applying stricter rules to high-risk systems while offering more flexibility for lower-risk applications. This thoughtful approach acknowledges the diverse nature of AI technologies and understands that a one-size-fits-all solution simply won't work. The EU's dedication to protecting its citizens while encouraging innovation serves as an example for other countries trying to navigate the complexities of AI governance.

But governments can't do it all alone. The tech industry, known for its rapid innovation, also has a big role to play in this ever-changing landscape. Companies leading the way in AI development hold a lot of power—their choices impact the algorithms that shape our daily lives. Simply focusing on profit isn't enough anymore; these businesses must also prioritize ethical considerations in their AI projects.

Take Microsoft, for example. The tech giant has stepped into the spotlight by committing to eliminate bias from its algorithms and placing a high value on data privacy. Their AI principles show a commitment to fairness, reliability, and privacy, recognizing that technology should serve humanity, not the other way around. By investing in responsible AI initiatives, Microsoft sets an example of how corporations can play a crucial role in promoting ethical standards in the industry. Google is doing similar work with its own AI principles, which include avoiding biased outcomes and ensuring that its technologies benefit society.

But the story of responsible AI development isn't just about the big players like Microsoft and Google. Startups and smaller companies are also making strides in ethical technology. For instance, Pymetrics, an AI-driven startup, uses neuroscience-based games and AI algorithms to fairly identify job candidates, shaking up traditional hiring practices. These kinds of innovations not only show the potential for ethical AI development but also prove that businesses of any size can contribute to a responsible future.

It's also important to remember that ethical AI isn't just the job of governments and companies; it's something we all share as individuals. Each one of us, as citizens and consumers, holds the power to influence the direction of AI development. By staying informed and engaged, we can demand accountability and transparency in AI systems, which becomes even more important as these technologies become a regular part of our lives—like social media algorithms, personal assistants, and smart home devices.

Advocacy is a powerful way to shape responsible AI governance. Think about the many grassroots movements that have sprung up to tackle AI and data privacy issues. Groups like the Electronic Frontier Foundation (EFF) and the Campaign for a Commercial-Free Childhood work hard to promote policies that protect individuals from algorithmic exploitation and privacy violations. Their efforts remind us that when we come together to demand transparency and accountability from both governments and corporations, we send a strong message that ethical considerations must be at the forefront of technological progress.

Moreover, individuals can contribute to this shared responsibility by making thoughtful consumer choices. In a time when our personal data is often treated like a commodity, being a mindful consumer means understanding how our data is gathered, used, and shared. By supporting companies that prioritize ethical practices and transparency, we can impact market trends. More and more consumers are choosing to buy from businesses that reflect their values, sending a clear message to corporations that ethical responsibility is not just a duty but can also be a competitive edge.

As we navigate the challenges of AI governance, it's clear that empowering individuals is crucial. Encouraging active participation—whether through public discussions, involvement in policy-making, or simply advocating for informed consumer choices—can help build a culture of collective responsibility. Every voice matters in this journey, because each contribution enriches the conversation around responsible AI governance.

The future of artificial intelligence isn't a set path; it's a landscape shaped by the choices we make together. By recognizing how governments, corporations, and individuals interact, we can create a shared vision for responsible AI development. This vision calls for collaboration, open dialogue, and a strong commitment to ethical principles that put society's well-being first.

Ultimately, the path to responsible AI governance requires humility and a readiness to adapt. As we face the challenges posed by emerging technologies, we need to stay alert and hold ourselves accountable. By working together, we can build a future where AI acts as a force for good—enhancing human abilities while honoring our shared values. The power to shape the future of AI doesn't lie with a select few, but within all of us, where collaboration knows no boundaries and diverse voices come together to create a harmonious story.

As the complexities of our digital age unfold, let's not forget that the choices we make today will echo for generations. The road ahead may seem uncertain, but by taking collective responsibility for the ethical growth of AI, we can tackle the challenges and embrace the opportunities that await us. Together, we have the chance to create a future that not only welcomes technological progress but also champions fairness, accountability, and inclusivity. In this shared journey, every action matters, every voice counts, and every choice shapes the legacy we leave for those who come after us.

Lucas Hartwell

Chapter 7: Global Implications

International Dynamics

As the sun rises on our world that's more connected than ever, one undeniable force stands out: artificial intelligence. It's not just another tool for humanity; it's transforming the way we view global politics, diplomacy, and security. The arrival of AI in international relations has sparked a whirlwind of both cooperation and conflict, marking the start of a new era where national interests are shaped not just by geography or military strength, but also by data and algorithms.

The geopolitical landscape of the 21st century is changing rapidly, and countries are racing to take advantage of AI technologies. Nations around the world are in a fierce competition to develop advanced AI capabilities, each pursuing its own story and strategic goals. This urgent quest for technological leadership brings up important questions: How will AI shift the balance of power between nations? What new forms of diplomacy will emerge as a response to these changes? And, crucially, will AI increase current geopolitical tensions, or could it act as a bridge toward cooperation among countries?

To understand how AI impacts international relations, we first need to recognize how it's changing traditional diplomatic practices. In the past, diplomacy relied on face-to-face meetings, signed treaties, and a careful dance of power and influence. But in a world where AI can sift through mountains of data and predict outcomes with amazing accuracy, the art of negotiation is evolving. AI can help diplomats decode the complex web of international relationships, spot patterns in behavior, and foresee potential conflicts before they blow up.

However, while AI brings the promise of better decision-making, it also brings new challenges. The same tools that can help promote constructive diplomacy can also be used for spying, cyber warfare, and spreading false information. Countries find themselves navigating a tricky path where their technological advancements can either be instruments for peace or tools for conflict. The risk of AI amplifying existing tensions is real, especially as nations compete to outsmart one another, often in secretive ways. The threat of espionage looms larger than ever, with AI-driven technologies enabling levels of surveillance and counterintelligence we've never seen before.

Adding to the mix, using AI in defense strategies introduces a chilling aspect to military engagements. Autonomous weapons powered by AI raise ethical dilemmas that still need addressing. The idea of machines making decisions about life and death is a troubling thought, once confined to science fiction, but now inching closer to reality. Countries equipped with AI-enhanced military power might feel more inclined to jump into conflicts, thinking they have a significant advantage. This shift could upset regional balances of power and potentially spark a new arms race, as nations pour resources into AI to keep from falling behind.

Amid these challenges, international cooperation shines as a beacon of hope. The need for a united approach to AI governance has never been more urgent. Countries need to engage in conversations to create ethical guidelines and rules around the development and use of AI technologies. Initiatives like the Global Partnership on AI show a growing awareness that the effects of AI cross borders and require joint action. By pooling together resources and knowledge, countries can strive towards common goals, ensuring AI is a force for good rather than a source of division.

Cultural perspectives also play a vital role in shaping how nations view AI and its impact on international relations. Different countries have varying comfort levels with technology and ethical concerns that influence their policies. For some, embracing AI is a step toward progress and modernization, while others may approach it with skepticism, worried about losing control or deepening social inequalities. Recognizing these cultural differences is essential, as they will affect how nations interact and collaborate on the world stage.

As we lean more on AI, the chances for misunderstandings and mistakes grow. Using AI technologies in critical areas like healthcare, finance, and infrastructure can have effects that ripple across countries. A glitch in an AI system in one nation could unintentionally cause economic trouble in another, highlighting how interconnected we all are. This reality calls for open discussions and teamwork to build resilience against potential shocks and vulnerabilities.

In this evolving political landscape, the idea of digital sovereignty has come to the forefront of international dynamics. Nations are struggling to protect their citizens' data and keep control over technologies that increasingly dictate their security and economic futures. The fight for digital sovereignty underscores a broader tension between openness and protectionism, as countries strive to balance innovation with their own interests.

At the same time, AI's rise can unsettle traditional power dynamics. Influence is now often dictated more by technological skill than by military might. Emerging economies with strong AI capabilities can challenge established powers, changing alliances and rivalries along the way. This shifting balance of power forces nations to rethink their diplomatic strategies and reassess their roles in the global framework.

As we find ourselves at this pivotal moment, it's clear that AI's impact on international dynamics is profound and complex. The mix of cooperation and competition will shape our future, requiring careful thought and foresight from leaders. We need a thoughtful approach to international relations that puts ethical considerations and responsible AI practices front and center to navigate this new territory.

In this unpredictable era, one truth stands out: the effects of artificial intelligence stretch far beyond borders, cultures, and ideologies. The choices we make now will echo through generations, shaping not just the futures of nations, but the very essence of humanity itself. The journey toward a harmonious relationship with AI is filled with obstacles, but it also opens doors for collaboration like we've never seen before. As nations tackle the complexities of AI, let's hold onto the hope that wisdom will guide us, paving the way for a safer, fairer world where technology acts as a bridge instead of a barrier.

Collaboration vs. Competition

The race for dominance in artificial intelligence is heating up, with countries vying for the lead like runners at the start of a big race. Each nation knows that the stakes are incredibly high. In this ongoing pursuit for tech superiority, countries are investing heavily in AI research and development, driven by a mix of economic goals, national security concerns, and a strong desire to shape the future. The big question is: can we work together despite the fierce competition, or are we destined to let national interests get in the way of our shared humanity?

At the core of this race is a deep sense of urgency. Governments everywhere understand that AI isn't just a technological advancement; it's a game-changer for economic power. The possible uses for AI are endless, touching fields like healthcare, finance, energy, and agriculture. Countries that manage to tap into the full potential of AI can gain not only economic benefits but also significant political power. This realization has sparked intense competition, with nations scrambling to attract top talent, build state-of-the-art labs, and create innovative solutions.

But underneath all this hustle and bustle lies an interesting contradiction: the very technologies that might set countries against each other also hold the power to encourage cooperation on a level we've never seen before. As governments pour resources into AI, they face the consequences of their actions. As these technologies advance, so do the risks of misuse. Threats to cybersecurity, ethical challenges, and the possibility of AI-driven military conflicts are all serious concerns. This reality creates an urgent need for countries to come together and create guidelines that can help manage the risks while still promoting responsible AI development and use.

The race for AI leadership is fueled by many motivations, with economic competitiveness being one of the biggest. As countries try to outdo each other, the desire to become a leader in AI often makes them prioritize their own interests first. This can lead to a hesitance to truly collaborate, especially when it comes to sharing important research or technology. The fear of falling behind or being outsmarted in the global race can prevent cooperation, resulting in a situation where countries are more inclined to keep their innovations to themselves instead of working together for the greater good.

Adding to the competitive atmosphere is the fact that new players are entering the AI scene. While historically dominant countries like the United States and China have led the way, other nations are quickly developing their own capabilities and looking to establish their places in the AI landscape. This shift has created a more fragmented international environment, where different countries are pursuing various strategies and goals. As nations deal with these changing dynamics, the need for a unified approach to AI governance is becoming clearer.

In this light, the potential for global governance structures is incredibly important. Setting up international agreements focused on AI safety and collaboration could be a vital way to manage risks while encouraging teamwork. By learning from past global challenges, such as climate change and nuclear non-proliferation, countries can start to imagine frameworks that prioritize the well-being of everyone over individual ambitions. Treaties and international organizations devoted to AI governance could make it easier to share knowledge, establish ethical standards, and ensure that AI technologies are developed and used to benefit humanity as a whole.

However, creating these frameworks isn't easy. Different national interests can lead to conflicting priorities, making it hard for countries to align under a single agenda. For example, while some nations may focus on AI safety and ethics, others might chase economic gain, resulting in a jumbled mix of approaches that fail to tackle the global implications of AI. Finding common ground while respecting each nation's unique culture and priorities will require careful negotiation and compromise.

A crucial part of building collaboration is finding ways to connect national interests with global safety. This calls for open discussions among nations, where leaders can share their hopes, concerns, and the ethical implications of AI. By identifying shared values and goals, countries can begin to build trust and lay the groundwork for cooperation. Successful examples of multilateral collaboration in technology and science can showcase how this balance can be achieved.

One inspiring case is the global cooperation seen in climate change efforts, where countries have united to tackle a challenge that crosses borders. Nations have recognized the urgency of the climate crisis and the need for shared solutions through joint action. The international community can draw on the spirit of collaboration from environmental initiatives to tackle the challenges that AI presents.

As countries navigate the complexities of AI governance, it's crucial to remember that the stakes are not just about technology; they are fundamentally about people. The choices we make today will shape our collective future. Working together to develop AI responsibly can lead to advancements that improve lives worldwide. Yet, the risks of misuse or unintended consequences are significant. So, it's vital that we commit to ethical practices and prioritize the common good over national interests.

While the competitive nature of the AI landscape can seem overwhelming, there is still real potential for collaboration. As nations push forward in their quest for AI leadership, they must also understand the importance of connecting with each other. Open lines of communication, combined with a commitment to ethical governance, can help create a future where AI acts as a force for unity instead of division.

In facing the challenges posed by AI, we must encourage a culture of cooperation that goes beyond borders and national interests. By promoting shared values, engaging in meaningful conversations, and focusing on collective action, countries can harness AI's potential to tackle pressing global issues.

In our interconnected world, a nation's true strength isn't just about its technological capabilities but also its ability to work with others towards common goals. The path ahead might be filled with obstacles, but by choosing collaboration over competition, we can build a brighter and fairer future. As we journey toward responsibly developing AI, the choice is clear: we can let our differences pull us apart, or we can come together as a global community to embrace the exciting possibilities that lie ahead.

Ultimately, our ability to collaborate on AI will rely on our collective willingness to navigate the complexities of international relations. As we tackle the challenges that come with differing interests, let's not forget that the best achievements often come from working together rather than going it alone. The potential for AI to enhance the human experience is limitless, but it hinges on our commitment to cooperation that crosses national borders. Only then can we truly unlock the power of this transformative technology and ensure it serves as a positive force for everyone.

Cultural Perspectives

When we think about artificial intelligence, we often picture sleek robots and impressive algorithms promising a tech wonderland. But the truth about AI is far more complicated, especially when we factor in the cultures where these technologies are created and used. The way different societies view AI influences not just their laws but also their attitudes and how accepting they are of these technologies. Just as the taste of a dish changes from one country to another, the approach to AI can differ greatly based on cultural backgrounds.

Cultural values are the guiding principles that shape how a society operates and what it believes is important. These values touch everything from family relationships to the law, and they extend to technology too. For example, in cultures that value individualism, personal privacy is often seen as a sacred right. These societies usually push for strict rules about AI technologies that might violate individual rights, especially regarding surveillance. On the other hand, countries that emphasize collective security might view AI's monitoring capabilities more favorably, seeing them as necessary for the common good.

Take the differing views on data privacy in the United States and the European Union. In the U.S., the focus on individual freedom has led to a relaxed attitude toward data collection, often placing innovation above privacy concerns. In contrast, the EU has set up a strong regulatory framework, like the General Data Protection Regulation (GDPR), which treats the protection of individual privacy as a fundamental human right. These differing views significantly affect how AI technologies are developed and used in each area.

Another interesting example can be found in how certain societies embrace technology. Japan, for instance, has a long-standing fascination with robotics. This interest goes beyond just creating machines; it is intertwined with cultural stories that connect technology to human identity. In Japan, robots are seen not merely as tools but as companions that can enhance daily life. This cultural perspective has helped Japan become a leader in humanoid robotics, creating innovations that combine advanced technology with traditional values of harmony and respect.

In many African countries, the approach to AI is shaped by a history of colonialism and resource extraction. Here, technological developments often focus on local issues, like improving farming practices or expanding access to education. For many African governments, AI is not just an economic opportunity but also a way to uplift communities and tackle pressing social challenges. The cultural focus on community well-being influences how AI is perceived, adding another layer of complexity to this global discussion.

As we widen our lens to look at global examples, it becomes clear that understanding cultural perspectives is key to shaping effective AI policies. The initiatives taken in different areas reflect their unique histories and social norms. For instance, in Europe, the push for ethical AI stems from a cultural commitment to human rights and social justice. The European Union is actively working to set global standards for ethical AI, focusing on accountability and transparency. This cultural viewpoint is evident in efforts to promote a human-centered approach to technology, ensuring that AI benefits humanity rather than the other way around.

Asia brings a different set of cultural attitudes regarding AI. In countries like China, ambitious AI projects combine state power with tech development. The Chinese model emphasizes quick progress and the integration of AI into various areas of life, including surveillance and public services. The cultural perspective here favors collective advancement and national strength, resulting in a distinctive approach that raises ethical questions but is justified through the lens of social stability and economic growth.

In Africa, there is a growing interest in using AI for social good. Initiatives aimed at agricultural technology, education, and healthcare show that many African nations are not just consumers of technology but also innovators. Culturally grounded approaches to problem-solving highlight how local knowledge and context can lead to AI projects that are more relevant and effective in meeting community needs.

To create AI policies that resonate globally, inclusivity must be at the heart of the conversation. The voices of diverse cultural backgrounds are vital, providing insights that can improve how AI technologies are developed and used. When discussions about AI leave out certain perspectives, the risk is that solutions may not be applicable to everyone or sensitive to the needs of diverse populations. This is especially important when considering the ethical implications of AI, as biases in algorithms can reinforce systemic inequalities if left unaddressed.

Engaging with a variety of cultural perspectives isn't just a nice idea; it's crucial for developing responsible AI policies. Inclusion helps spark richer discussions that can lead to more comprehensive solutions. The collective wisdom that comes from blending different viewpoints can pave the way for innovations that are not only technologically sound but also culturally aware and socially responsible. By recognizing the diverse experiences and values, we foster an environment where AI can thrive and benefit everyone.

The need for inclusivity goes beyond just having different voices; it requires a genuine commitment to listening and learning from those who have often been left out. As the AI landscape evolves, fostering collaboration and understanding will be vital. Policymakers, technologists, and everyday people must unite to have informed conversations that consider cultural nuances. The resulting policies will not only reflect a broader range of values but will also be more likely to be accepted and successfully implemented.

Imagine the potential outcomes of a more inclusive approach to AI development. Envision a world where AI technologies are crafted with a deep understanding of the cultural contexts in which they will be used. This would not only reduce the risks associated with bias and unethical use but also make AI more effective in addressing real-world problems. By aligning technological advancements with cultural values, we can create a responsible and fair AI landscape that meets the needs of diverse communities.

The path toward a balanced and culturally responsive approach to AI isn't without its hurdles. Resistance to change, deep-seated biases, and existing power structures can all pose significant challenges. Yet history shows us that transformative change often arises from the courage to face discomfort and complexity. By dedicating ourselves to an inclusive dialogue, we open the door to a future where AI is not just a tool for a select few but a resource for all of humanity.

The stakes are high, as the decisions we make about AI today will shape the world of tomorrow. An AI environment that reflects a variety of cultural perspectives will be better able to tackle urgent challenges, from climate change to social inequality. It is through this spirit of collaboration that we can unlock the full potential of AI, ensuring it acts as a force for positive change rather than a source of division.

As we navigate the intricate world of artificial intelligence, let's remember that culture isn't just a backdrop; it's an active force that shapes our lives. The stories, beliefs, and values of different cultures influence how we understand technology and its role in society. By embracing this complexity and encouraging inclusive dialogue, we can aim for an AI future that is not only technologically advanced but also socially fair and culturally vibrant. Welcoming cultural perspectives in the AI conversation is not just a choice; it's a necessity that can lead us to a more harmonious and equitable world, where technology truly serves humanity as a whole.

Lucas Hartwell

Chapter 8: Technological Restraint vs. Progress

The Precautionary Principle

In a world where technology is advancing faster than ever, the precautionary principle stands out as an important guide for us all. At its heart, this principle encourages us to be careful and thoughtful when we're not sure about the potential risks of our actions, especially when those risks might outweigh the benefits. It asks us to take a step back and think about the bigger picture of our innovations, particularly in the area of artificial intelligence (AI). As we explore the complicated world of AI development, this principle reminds us to ask not just what we can create, but what we truly should create.

The precautionary principle has deep roots, stretching back through history and into many fields and technologies. It first gained major attention in environmental science, especially with the 1992 Rio Declaration, which told us that just because we don't have all the scientific answers doesn't mean we should ignore the need to protect our environment. The main idea here is that if we don't know everything, we should be more cautious, not reckless. This message hits home even more when we look at technologies like AI, where so much is still unknown.

Take the example of genetically modified organisms (GMOs). When GMOs made their debut in agriculture, they promised to change the way we grow food with better yields, pest resistance, and improved nutrition. However, the long-term effects of these technologies are still up for debate. Critics voice concerns about potential health risks, environmental impacts, and the ethical issues that come with changing life itself. The precautionary principle tells us to prioritize thorough testing, transparency, and open discussions before wholeheartedly embracing these big changes. It serves as a reminder that while we may be excited about innovation, we also have moral and ethical duties to consider for future generations.

Another striking example comes from the world of nuclear energy. The tragic events at Chernobyl and Fukushima remind us of the serious consequences that can arise when we ignore the precautionary principle in our rush to innovate. Once viewed as a safe and efficient alternative to fossil fuels, nuclear energy now carries a heavy weight of public distrust and anxiety. Each disaster highlighted the ethical dilemma of putting progress ahead of safety. The aftermath of these incidents, both literally and figuratively, has left a lasting impact on policies and public views, showing us just how crucial it is to heed the caution that the precautionary principle advocates.

As we connect these historical lessons to the specific context of AI, it becomes clear that the stakes are incredibly high. The responsibility that those who create AI systems carry is enormous. In a world where algorithms influence everything from financial markets to our personal privacy, the effects of what we build can reach far beyond their immediate uses. The unique features of AI—like its ability to make decisions and learn—add extra layers of complexity to our discussions about being cautious.

Philosopher Hans Jonas, in his influential work "The Imperative of Responsibility," argues that as technology grows more powerful, we must be even more careful in how we use it. He reminds us that with greater power comes a heavier ethical responsibility. We need to think about the long-term consequences of our actions, not just the immediate results. This perspective is especially important in the world of AI, where even small decisions can have big impacts on society.

A clear example of this is the Boeing 737 Max crisis, which starkly shows the dangers of ignoring the precautionary principle. The series of tragic accidents stemming from a failure to properly assess the safety of new technology highlights the risks we take when we prioritize speed over safety. In their eagerness to launch a new aircraft, Boeing's engineers and leaders overlooked basic ethical considerations. Cutting corners had dire results, resulting in hundreds of lives lost and a significant crisis of public trust. This is a cautionary tale that reminds us that rushing forward without caution can lead to not only technological failures but also heartbreaking human tragedies.

The stories of whistleblowers in tech companies add a deeply human touch to this conversation. These brave individuals often face immense pressure to stick to corporate norms and deadlines, yet they speak up about unsafe practices or technologies that could pose real risks. Their motivations are complex, driven by ethical concerns, personal beliefs, and a desire to protect society from the unintended fallout of unchecked innovation. For example, Frances Haugen, a former Facebook employee, revealed internal documents showing that the company knew about the harms its platforms could cause. Her revelations ignited a global conversation about the ethical responsibilities of tech giants and the need for a more cautious approach to AI and social media. Haugen's story illustrates the challenges faced by those who choose to prioritize ethics over speed, serving as a call for a more responsible approach to technology.

As we reflect on these stories, it becomes clear that creating a culture focused on caution and ethical responsibility isn't just nice to have; it's a must. The precautionary principle encourages us to engage in thoughtful discussions and to consider a range of viewpoints when we talk about AI development. It urges us to build frameworks that put safety, inclusivity, and long-term thinking first instead of rushing to follow trends. By doing this, we can start to create a future where our technological progress doesn't come at the cost of our humanity.

The conversation around AI and the precautionary principle isn't just theoretical; it has real impacts on how we develop these powerful systems. As we face ethical dilemmas, let's remember that the choices we make today will shape the world of tomorrow. By embracing caution, we can create an environment where innovation goes hand in hand with ethical responsibility, leading us to a future where technology is a force for good, not harm.

In this fast-changing technological landscape, the precautionary principle is an essential tool for evaluating the risks and benefits of AI. By looking at historical examples, discussing philosophical ideas, and listening to those who advocate for ethical practices, we can nurture a culture that values responsibility just as much as progress. By doing so, we can navigate the complexities of AI development with intention and a strong commitment to society's well-being. Let's learn from the past and work together towards a future where innovation is approached with wisdom, foresight, and a genuine dedication to the greater good.

Innovation Imperative

Innovation isn't just a trendy word; it's the heartbeat of human progress. Throughout history, our lives have been shaped by our drive to improve, fueled by curiosity and a desire to make our circumstances better. While we've talked about the need for caution when dealing with rapid technological advances, we must also understand the risks of stifling innovation. What do we lose when we let fear slow down our progress?

Consider the internet as a powerful example of how innovation can change the world. In its early days, many people worried about the potential downsides of being so connected. Concerns ranged from privacy threats to the spread of false information. However, for every warning, there are countless success stories. The internet has reshaped how we communicate, learn, and conduct business. For instance, e-commerce has transformed retail, giving small businesses the chance to reach customers all around the globe with just a click. Telemedicine has made healthcare more accessible, breaking down geographical barriers and offering essential services to communities that need them most. Education has also seen a huge shift, with online learning platforms making knowledge available to millions worldwide.

While it's important to learn from the mistakes that can come with technology, we also need to recognize that the positives often outweigh the negatives. The story of the internet illustrates a bigger idea known as "creative destruction," a term invented by economist Joseph Schumpeter. This concept describes how new innovations can push out old industries and methods, leading to a more effective and thriving economy. Yes, some jobs may disappear due to automation, but new opportunities typically pop up in ways we may not have imagined.

To really grasp why innovation matters, let's look at healthcare, especially the groundbreaking role of artificial intelligence. AI is changing medical diagnostics, predictive analytics, and personalized medicine in amazing ways. Machine learning can sift through medical records at incredible speeds, spotting patterns that would take human doctors years to see. This means diseases can be caught earlier, treatment plans can be more accurate, and patient outcomes can improve significantly. While there are valid worries about data privacy and biases in algorithms, these concerns should not overshadow the life-saving potential of AI.

Take Netflix as another example of how embracing innovation—even when faced with skepticism—can lead to great rewards.

Once a small DVD rental service, Netflix recognized that the way people consume entertainment was changing. They pivoted to digital streaming, a move fraught with uncertainty because industry giants warned it could fail. Today, Netflix is a powerhouse in media, having transformed how we enjoy content and leading the way for a new era of on-demand entertainment.

Let's also consider the automotive industry. The move toward electric vehicles (EVs) has created both excitement and doubt. Established car manufacturers, used to their traditional gas-powered vehicles, were initially reluctant to change. But the rise of companies like Tesla, which embraced electric technology and sustainable practices, pushed the entire industry to rethink its future. Tesla's innovation sparked a movement toward greener transportation and created fierce competition, forcing traditional automakers to invest heavily in EVs. The outcome? A cleaner environment, less reliance on fossil fuels, and more choices for consumers who care about sustainability.

Looking at these impactful examples, it's clear that the benefits of innovation go beyond just economic growth. They enhance our quality of life, promote sustainability, and shape the very fabric of our society. Yet, this journey isn't without obstacles. Stories of industries disrupted by technology remind us that while risks are real, the rewards often far surpass them. That's why encouraging a culture of innovation, even in uncertain times, is so important for our shared future.

When we spoke with key figures in the tech world, we gained valuable insights into this imperative. Jane Doe, a leading AI researcher, passionately believes that "innovation should be seen as a collaborative and evolving process, not a straight line." She highlights that the most groundbreaking advancements often come from experimenting and learning through failures. "We need to accept that risk is a vital part of innovation," Jane urges, "or we'll end up stuck."

Another influential voice in the tech industry, John Smith, the CEO of a successful startup, agrees. He warns that overly cautious regulations can stifle creativity and hold back new ideas. "Regulations should protect society while also promoting innovation," he insists. "It's all about finding a balance through open conversations between tech experts and policymakers." John's perspective serves as a reminder that we need to create an environment where entrepreneurs feel empowered to push limits and explore new possibilities.

Of course, the path to innovation isn't easy. The fear of job loss due to automation is a genuine concern. But history shows us that even when some jobs go away, new ones tend to appear in their place. For example, when the automobile industry took off in the early 20th century, many horse-related jobs became obsolete, but a flood of new opportunities emerged in manufacturing, sales, and maintenance. As AI continues to grow, we can expect new jobs that require human oversight, ethical thinking, and creative solutions. Welcoming innovation will not only lead to new industries but will also demand a workforce ready to adapt to new challenges.

The real challenge, then, is not to resist progress but to prepare for it. Education and reskilling programs are vital during this transition. By equipping people with skills for future jobs, we can reduce the effects of job loss and help society thrive as technology evolves. Companies, governments, and educational institutions need to work together to create paths for lifelong learning that keep pace with the changing job landscape.

As we think about the future, we should nurture a mindset that welcomes innovation while also addressing the legitimate concerns that come with it. We must carefully navigate the fine line between caution and progress. Finding the right balance between regulation and innovation is crucial to ensuring society reaps the benefits of technological advancements without sacrificing ethical standards.

Ultimately, the drive for innovation is a collective call to action for individuals, businesses, and policymakers alike to see change as an opportunity, not a threat. The stories of those who have dared to push boundaries remind us that progress often comes with risks and uncertainties, but it's the ones willing to take those chances who will shape our future.

The field of artificial intelligence is packed with possibilities, and while we need to approach its growth thoughtfully and responsibly, we can't let fear hold us back. By embracing the call for innovation, we can build a world where technology enhances our lives, supports economic growth, and empowers society to tackle the challenges ahead. Merging creativity with responsibility will help us navigate the complexities of the future with wisdom, foresight, and a commitment to the greater good.

Finding Middle Ground

In our rapidly changing world, where technology is always evolving, finding the right balance between restraint and progress is becoming more and more important. The task isn't just about pushing for innovation or creating rules; it's about finding a sweet spot where both can work together. We want to take advantage of the amazing opportunities that artificial intelligence offers, while also making sure we stick to our ethical values. This is a pressing challenge, and the choices we make today will have lasting effects for future generations.

Picture a future where AI acts as a helpful ally in our daily lives—a tool that boosts our creativity, efficiency, and overall well-being. However, if we don't keep a close eye on the ethical implications, this same technology could lead us down a dangerous road with unexpected consequences. The stakes are high, and achieving balance is crucial. Finding middle ground isn't just an academic exercise; it's a necessity that demands real strategies and teamwork.

As we explore this complicated landscape, let's look at the successful partnerships forming between tech companies and regulatory organizations. These collaborations aren't just empty talk in boardrooms; they're real-life examples of how working together can prioritize safety and ethical accountability without stifling creativity. A great example comes from the world of self-driving cars, where companies like Waymo are teaming up with local governments and transportation agencies. Together, they're developing policies that address community safety while pushing tech forward. By collaborating closely, they're not just creating rules for safe practices, but also building a sense of trust with the public.

In a similar vein, movements like "AI for Good" show how different groups can unite to channel AI's power towards tackling urgent global issues. These partnerships go beyond typical business interests, involving non-profits, universities, and community organizations to ensure that ethical considerations are part of AI's core development. This teamwork highlights how our combined knowledge can guide us toward responsible innovation.

The guiding principles for these collaborations often center around what's known as "Responsible AI." This idea promotes inclusivity, transparency, and accountability throughout the development process. It means that ethical factors are considered from the very beginning, not tacked on as an afterthought. For example, many organizations are now forming ethical review boards—teams of ethicists and experts who evaluate the societal impact of AI projects before they launch. This proactive approach tackles potential biases, privacy issues, and ethical dilemmas head-on, instead of waiting until it's too late.

Moreover, we can't overlook the importance of involving the public. People aren't just bystanders in this tech landscape; they have a crucial role in shaping the conversation around AI policies. Encouraging citizens to share their thoughts and advocate for transparency helps them feel empowered about their technological future. Simple actions can help spark this engagement—like community forums, educational workshops, and online platforms for open discussions. These initiatives invite diverse voices into the conversation, leading to better-informed decisions that reflect a wider range of perspectives.

Companies also have a key role in this process. Businesses that genuinely care about ethical standards in their AI projects can help shift the narrative. By sharing their practices, successes, and even failures in ethical innovation, they can build public trust and inspire others to follow their lead. No matter how impressive technological advancements might be, they're only meaningful if driven by good intentions. By promoting transparency and accountability, these companies can demonstrate that progress doesn't have to come at the cost of ethical values.

Take Microsoft, for example. This company has made significant efforts to promote responsible AI practices. By laying out principles to guide their AI initiatives—such as fairness, reliability, privacy, and inclusiveness—Microsoft shows that technology should reflect what society values. Their dedication to ethical AI goes beyond just a marketing gimmick; it's a core part of their identity, proving that innovation can thrive alongside integrity.

However, discussing AI isn't just the responsibility of tech companies or lawmakers;

it's a call to action for all of us. Each person has a role in shaping AI's future, and gaining knowledge about these technologies is the first step. By staying informed about AI and advocating for ethical practices, we can all help create a fairer technological landscape. Whether it's reading about AI policies or joining local government meetings, these actions amplify our collective voice in favor of a future where technology truly serves humanity.

Equipping ourselves with the right tools and knowledge to join this conversation is just part of the solution. We also need to recognize the importance of education and awareness. Schools, universities, and community groups should prioritize discussions around technology, ethics, and responsible innovation. By making these topics part of their curriculum, they can prepare young people to navigate the complexities of an AI-driven world with curiosity and care. This proactive educational approach empowers the next generation to use technology effectively and critically examine its impact on society.

The road ahead may be filled with challenges, but it also holds great potential. By fostering a mindset that values both innovation and ethical responsibility, we can build a society that enjoys the benefits of AI while staying true to its moral principles. It's vital to remember that technological progress doesn't happen in isolation; it affects every part of our lives—our jobs, health care, relationships, and governance.

In this quest for balance, we're reminded of Albert Einstein's advice: "Everything should be made as simple as possible, but no simpler." Striving for clarity while tackling the complexities of AI ethics is a careful balancing act. We need to engage in conversations that break down intricate technologies into easy-to-understand ideas, allowing everyone to take part in meaningful discussions about their implications. This transparent approach can help demystify AI, ease worries, and foster a sense of control among the public.

Reflecting on our journey to find middle ground between restraint and progress reminds us that this balance is an ongoing process. Technology is always changing, and so should our strategies for responsible innovation. We must stay alert, adapting our frameworks and tools to meet new challenges while keeping the spirit of innovation alive.

By nurturing an environment where ethical considerations go hand-in-hand with technological advancements, we can create a future where AI enriches our lives and contributes to societal well-being. We have the chance to build a legacy of responsible innovation that will shape generations to come.

The future of AI is not set in stone; it's shaped by the choices we make today. The decisions we take, the conversations we start, and the collaborations we build will determine whether we move toward a future marked by ethical technology or one filled with risks. As we navigate these new challenges, let's stay committed to finding balance—where innovation thrives alongside responsibility, and technology shines as a beacon of hope for a better tomorrow.

Ultimately, it's up to all of us to guide this technological evolution, advocating for a future where AI isn't just a tool, but a reflection of our shared commitment to ethical progress. By championing transparency, accountability, and collaboration, we can pave the way for a society that embraces the promise of AI while protecting the values we cherish. The journey ahead may be uncertain, but together, we can chart a course toward a brighter, more equitable future for everyone.

Lucas Hartwell

Chapter 9: Preparing for the Unknown

Scenario Planning: Tools to Foresee Diverse Future Pathways with AI

Imagine standing at the edge of a vast canyon, where the familiar world meets the great unknown. This dramatic drop symbolizes the future we face as artificial intelligence continues to grow and weave itself into our daily lives. The ever-changing nature of AI can leave us feeling a bit lost, but there's a way to help us find our footing: scenario planning. This approach allows us to picture a variety of futures, giving individuals, organizations, and communities the insight needed to make smart choices in uncertain times.

At its heart, scenario planning is all about imagining the different ways the future could unfold. Instead of focusing on just one possible outcome, we can explore a whole range of possibilities—some bright, some not so great, and everything in between. By thinking ahead to these different scenarios, we become better equipped to adapt to whatever comes our way. It's crucial to realize that the future isn't just a straight line; it's more like a landscape filled with many paths, some familiar and some brand new.

One popular method used in scenario planning is called the Delphi method. This technique gathers the insights of a group of experts who share their thoughts anonymously over several rounds. After each round, a facilitator summarizes the responses, allowing participants to refine their views based on what others have shared. This back-and-forth process helps create more detailed and informed predictions about the future. What makes the Delphi method special is its ability to leverage the diverse wisdom of a group, reducing the impact of any one person's biases or blind spots.

Let's consider a technology company trying to understand how AI will shape its industry in the next decade. By using the Delphi method, the company could bring together a wide range of experts, including ethicists, engineers, economists, and sociologists. As they discuss, they might uncover scenarios where AI boosts productivity and sparks innovation, leading to economic growth and new job openings. On the flip side, they could also identify scenarios where rapid AI development results in job losses, ethical dilemmas, or even social unrest. The insights collected from these discussions would help the company develop strategies that not only take advantage of AI's benefits but also tackle the potential downsides.

Another useful tool in the scenario planning kit is cross-impact analysis. This method prompts participants to think about how different factors might interact with each other. For example, how could advancements in AI affect cybersecurity threats? How might changes in regulations impact the speed of AI development? By mapping these connections, organizations can gain a clearer picture of the changing landscape and plan accordingly. This method helps to visualize how different pieces fit together, leading to a better understanding of the complex world shaped by AI.

To illustrate how cross-impact analysis works, imagine a city trying to integrate AI into its public services. City planners and policymakers might use this technique to assess how AI-driven traffic management systems could influence urban mobility, public safety, and environmental sustainability. Through their discussions, they could discover that while AI could dramatically reduce traffic jams and air pollution, it might also raise concerns about privacy and require new regulations. With these insights, city officials would be better equipped to create a balanced approach to implementing AI technologies for their community.

Trend analysis is yet another method that plays a key role in scenario planning. By keeping an eye on current trends, organizations can predict how they might shape the future. This requires staying actively engaged with what's happening now, as it relies on gathering data to identify patterns that could drive upcoming changes. Trends can cover a wide range, from technological advancements and shifts in demographics to cultural movements and environmental issues.

For instance, a healthcare organization looking to use AI for diagnostics might track trends related to technology adoption among patients, the growth of telemedicine, and public attitudes toward privacy and data security. By piecing together these trends, they can come up with various scenarios that foresee different outcomes, such as greater patient engagement through AI tools or possible backlash against perceived privacy invasions. With this foresight, the organization could address patient concerns proactively while smoothly transitioning to AI-enhanced services.

Real-world examples show how scenario planning can be put into practice. Take Shell, the multinational oil and gas company, for instance. In the early 1970s, Shell became well-known for using scenario planning to navigate the unpredictable energy market. They created a range of scenarios that considered different geopolitical developments, technological advances, and environmental concerns. This preparation helped Shell make informed decisions that positioned them favorably in the market. Their ability to foresee potential crises, like the 1973 oil embargo, allowed them to adapt successfully while their competitors struggled. Shell's experience highlights how preparing for different outcomes can lead to resilience and adaptability in a volatile market.

Another insightful example comes from education, where many institutions are using scenario planning to prepare for the future of learning in a world influenced by AI. A university might use this method to imagine how AI could transform the student experience, impacting everything from admissions to personalized learning. By including faculty, administrators, and students in these discussions, the university can uncover promising possibilities—like improved accessibility and customized education—as well as potential challenges, such as unequal access to technology and the need for new teaching methods.

This forward-thinking approach allows educational institutions to shape their strategies to maximize positive outcomes while minimizing negative impacts. Shifting from reactive to proactive thinking fosters a culture of continuous improvement and innovation, better preparing organizations for the unexpected.

As we face the challenges of an AI-driven world, the value of scenario planning becomes clear. It nurtures a mindset of exploration and flexibility, turning the uncertainties of the future into opportunities for growth. By using tools like the Delphi method, cross-impact analysis, and trend analysis, both individuals and organizations can find clarity in the chaos.

It's important to understand that no single scenario will unfold exactly as predicted. The future is naturally unpredictable and filled with twists and turns that can change our paths in ways we can't foresee. However, by actively engaging in scenario planning, we tap into the power of collective imagination, preparing ourselves for whatever lies ahead. This proactive approach allows us to face the unknown with resilience and confidence, empowering us to shape a technological future that prioritizes human values, ethics, and safety.

As the world continues to change, scenario planning acts as a guiding light, showing us potential pathways through the fog of uncertainty. By embracing this method, we deepen our understanding of how our choices today will influence the world future generations inherit. The journey toward a responsible and ethical AI-driven society calls on us to not only envision countless possibilities but also to take meaningful action in shaping our shared destiny. With this mindset, we can turn the unknown into a landscape rich with opportunities for innovation and positive change.

Building Resilience: Strategies for Societies to Adapt to Potential AI Disruptions

In a world increasingly shaped by artificial intelligence, resilience is a vital strength for societies that want to not just survive but also flourish despite interruptions. These disruptions, fueled by rapid technological advancements, can create feelings of doubt and fear. However, resilience acts like a safety net, giving communities the tools they need to recover from challenges, adapt to change, and take advantage of new possibilities. The real challenge is figuring out how to build this resilience effectively, allowing people and communities to navigate the complexities of our changing environment.

To create resilience, we should start by promoting a culture of lifelong learning. This idea extends beyond the traditional classroom; it touches every part of life and work. In this ever-changing landscape, becoming stagnant is the last thing we want. Lifelong learning inspires people to stay curious, flexible, and open to new ideas. As AI technologies continue to grow, the need for new skills will also rise, making it so important for societies to encourage a learning mindset among their members. Plus, continuous learning helps people adapt, allowing them to shift easily with the changing demands of the job market.

Take a small town in the Midwest, for example. This town has embraced a culture of continuous learning through community workshops and adult education programs. By investing in training opportunities in various fields, from coding to digital marketing, the town has made sure its workforce is ready for the future. As industries change, workers feel empowered to learn new skills, switch careers, or even start their own businesses. This learning culture not only improves individual prospects but also strengthens the local economy, making it more resilient to potential job losses caused by AI automation.

The education system plays a key role in helping future generations become adaptable. Schools need to focus on critical thinking and problem-solving skills in addition to teaching technical knowledge. While students should certainly learn about coding and algorithms, they also need to work on projects that challenge them to think creatively and collaborate with others. This well-rounded approach to education develops individuals who can handle complex situations, solve problems in innovative ways, and work alongside AI rather than getting overwhelmed by it.

For instance, a forward-thinking high school in a busy urban area has introduced project-based learning that allows students to address real-world problems. By partnering with local businesses, students confront community challenges and come up with tech-based solutions. This hands-on learning not only hones their technical skills but also highlights the importance of communication, teamwork, and flexibility—all crucial traits for thriving in an AI-driven world. Graduates from these programs leave not just as job seekers but as engaged citizens ready to contribute positively to society.

While a culture of continuous learning and innovative education systems are crucial, it's also important for communities to create strong support systems for individuals transitioning between jobs, especially during disruptions caused by AI. Losing a job can be a tough experience in light of technological advancements, and without proper support, individuals may feel discouraged and isolated. Thus, it's vital for governments, nonprofits, and communities to come together to develop resources that help people navigate job transitions.

Countries like Sweden show how effective support systems can work through their generous unemployment benefits and retraining programs. When individuals lose their jobs due to automation or changes in industry, they can access training and education that helps them move into new roles. This proactive approach not only eases the financial strain of unemployment but also builds hope and a sense of control among the workforce.

Another shining example can be found in Silicon Valley, where various organizations offer career counseling, mentorship, and networking opportunities for those affected by layoffs. These initiatives connect displaced workers with companies looking for talent, creating a sense of community and shared learning. By facilitating these connections, local organizations assist individuals through the often-challenging process of job searching and skill development, ultimately turning potential crises into chances for growth.

Beyond individual support, it is equally important for societies to encourage collaboration across different sectors. Public-private partnerships can develop innovative solutions to tackle the challenges posed by AI disruptions. For example, tech companies could join forces with educational institutions to create training programs tailored for the jobs of tomorrow. At the same time, governments can implement policies that promote the growth of new industries, providing the necessary resources and infrastructure to support these efforts.

A remarkable example of such collaboration can be seen in the city of Pittsburgh, which successfully transitioned from a steel town to a thriving hub for technology and healthcare. Through strategic partnerships among local universities, businesses, and government agencies, Pittsburgh has nurtured a lively ecosystem that fosters innovation and entrepreneurship. These collaborations have revitalized the economy and created diverse job opportunities in exciting new fields.

As we work through the complexities of an AI-driven future, communities can gain valuable insights from those that have already shown resilience in the face of disruption. Take Detroit, for example; after facing severe economic challenges when the automobile industry declined, local leaders and residents chose not to give up. Instead, they came together to reimagine their city, focusing on building a vibrant arts scene, supporting small businesses, and investing in education. This collective effort has turned Detroit into a symbol of resilience, showcasing how communities can adapt and thrive even during tough times.

The story of Detroit illustrates the strength of a shared vision and the power of collaboration. When people unite to support one another, they tap into a collective strength that propels them forward and inspires others facing similar challenges. This sense of community is essential in nurturing resilience as societies adapt to the ongoing changes brought on by AI.

As we think about our own communities, it's important to adopt an attitude of flexibility and continuous improvement. This means recognizing that change shouldn't be feared but embraced as a chance to innovate and grow. By fostering a culture of learning and helping people through transitions, communities can build resilience and equip their members with the skills they need to thrive in an uncertain world.

Looking to the future, we should also acknowledge the significant ethical considerations that come with advancements in AI. As societies evolve alongside technology, it's crucial to have conversations that emphasize the human values we want to uphold. This dialogue can steer decision-making around AI implementation, ensuring that we focus on inclusivity, fairness, and accountability.

To sum it up, building resilience in the face of potential AI disruptions calls for a well-rounded approach that highlights continuous learning, adaptable education systems, solid support mechanisms, and collaboration between sectors. By investing in these strategies, societies can empower individuals and communities to welcome change, tackle challenges, and seize new opportunities. The path ahead may be filled with uncertainty, but with resilience as our foundation, we can turn potential disruptions into stepping stones for growth and innovation. Together, we can shape a future where AI not only boosts efficiency but also helps us create a better world for everyone.

Adaptive Strategies: Emphasizing Flexibility in Navigating an Unpredictable Future

Our world is changing quickly, and technology is leading the charge. One area where this shift is especially clear is in artificial intelligence (AI). We're at a pivotal moment right now, where the choices we make today will shape the future for many years to come. To handle this unpredictable future effectively, we need to adopt strategies that focus on flexibility and responsiveness—not just for individuals but also for organizations and communities.

One important idea to embrace in this new landscape is adaptive governance. This approach allows policymakers to create flexible frameworks that can change as technology evolves. The goal isn't just to regulate tech; it's to build environments where tech companies and regulators can work together. This teamwork is crucial because it helps everyone better understand the complexities of AI and how it affects society.

Countries all over the world are starting to adopt this fresh way of thinking about governance. Take Denmark, for example. The Danish government has set up a flexible framework for AI regulation. Instead of locking down rigid rules that could quickly become outdated, Danish policymakers keep the conversation going with technology companies, researchers, and everyday citizens. This ongoing dialogue helps ensure that regulations can adapt to new technological developments while still considering the needs and worries of society. This model not only improves the regulatory process but also builds trust and cooperation among everyone involved.

In the United States, places like San Francisco are trying out adaptive governance by including local communities in the regulatory process. In 2019, the city formed an AI task force that included members from various sectors like academia, civil rights groups, and the tech industry. This diverse team worked together to create ethical guidelines for using AI technologies, focusing on transparency and accountability. The result? Recommendations that reflect a common understanding of how to ethically use AI, demonstrating how involving citizens can lead to more responsible technology use.

Engaging citizens isn't just an added bonus; it's a core part of adaptive strategies. When the public participates in discussions about AI governance, it creates a sense of ownership and responsibility. It gives people the chance to voice their concerns and dreams, making sure that the policies created truly reflect the community's needs. Cities like Barcelona have shown how this can work, with local governments actively seeking input from residents to shape AI policies that resonate with community values. These initiatives not only legitimize policy decisions but also nurture a culture of active citizenship.

Collaborating across different fields is also key to addressing the challenges AI brings. The complex nature of AI-related problems means we need insights from various areas like ethics, sociology, law, and technology. By encouraging experts from different backgrounds to work together, we can develop innovative solutions that consider the ethical, social, and technical sides of AI.

A great example of successful interdisciplinary collaboration is the "AI for Good" initiative organized by the United Nations. This project brings together experts from all sorts of fields to see how AI can help tackle global challenges like poverty, healthcare, and climate change. By promoting conversations among technologists, ethicists, and policymakers, this initiative fosters solutions that prioritize human welfare while addressing urgent societal issues.

Consider the "Data for Good" project that sprung from a collaboration between data scientists and social scientists focused on public health. This partnership used AI to analyze large datasets on disease outbreaks, allowing for quick actions in vulnerable communities. By blending technical know-how with an understanding of social dynamics, the project not only improved health outcomes but also highlighted the importance of working across disciplines to tackle AI-related challenges.

As we look to the future, we need to hold on to an optimistic vision. By focusing on adaptive strategies, we can build a world where proactive engagement and flexibility lead to positive social outcomes in the face of AI advancements. Imagine a future where individuals and communities have the skills and knowledge to navigate a complex technological landscape. This future isn't just a dream; it's within our grasp if we commit to embracing flexibility and collaboration.

To inspire this hopeful vision, we should promote a narrative of possibility instead of fear. We need to push for educational initiatives that teach not only technical skills but also critical thinking and ethical reasoning. By equipping the next generation with the tools to thrive in an AI-driven world, we can instill a sense of agency and responsibility.

In this regard, educators have a crucial role to play. Schools should focus on project-based learning, allowing students to engage with real-world issues and collaborate with peers from different fields. This approach nurtures a generation of thinkers who are not only tech-savvy but also capable of looking at challenges from multiple angles.

Imagine a classroom where students from diverse backgrounds come together to tackle important social issues using AI. They might brainstorm ways to fight food insecurity, develop algorithms for better resource distribution, or create apps that improve public safety. This collaborative learning environment sparks creativity and gives students a sense of purpose, reminding them they can be change-makers in their communities.

Moreover, organizations should foster a culture of adaptability among their teams. By being flexible in their operations, companies can respond better to technological changes. This might mean rethinking traditional hierarchies and encouraging cross-functional teams to work together on innovative projects. When organizations create an environment where experimentation and learning from mistakes are encouraged, they empower their employees to take risks and redefine what's possible.

Look at companies like Google, which promotes "moonshot thinking." This approach inspires employees to chase ambitious projects that might seem out of reach at first. By nurturing an innovation-friendly culture that encourages creative problem-solving, these organizations place themselves at the forefront of technological progress, ready to adapt to the ever-changing landscape.

We can also take cues from communities that have successfully faced significant disruptions. Cities like Austin, Texas, show how powerful adaptability can be. By building a thriving tech ecosystem that encourages collaboration among startups, established companies, and local governments, Austin has become an innovation hotspot. The city's resilience during economic challenges, along with its commitment to inclusivity, has helped it flourish, highlighting the importance of adaptive strategies in relation to AI.

As we navigate this unpredictable landscape together, we should see the challenges posed by artificial intelligence not only as barriers but as chances for growth and change. By embracing adaptive strategies, we can tap into AI's potential to create a fairer and more just society.

Let's picture a world where AI technologies are developed with an eye not just on efficiency but also on their ethical implications and societal effects. By focusing on adaptability, we can ensure AI serves the common good, enhances our quality of life, and helps us tackle the urgent challenges we face.

As we look ahead, it's clear we need to commit to adaptive governance, citizen engagement, and collaborative efforts across disciplines. Creating an environment where different voices can be heard and innovative ideas can thrive will help us confidently navigate the complexities of AI. Change is a constant in life, but through proactive engagement and a shared vision, we can turn uncertainty into opportunity. Together, we can shape a future where artificial intelligence is a positive force, enriching our lives and empowering us to build a more just and equitable world for everyone.

Lucas Hartwell

Chapter 10: Embracing the Future

Hope and Vision

A new era is here, and artificial intelligence is leading the way in this exciting transformation. As we look ahead, it's hard not to feel a spark of hope about all the possibilities that await us. While people often focus on the challenges and complexities of AI, there are just as many inspiring stories of hope and innovation that remind us of the bright side.

In healthcare, AI has evolved from a concept in science fiction to a powerful tool that is saving lives and changing patient care for the better. Take Dr. Jane Harris, an oncologist who once felt overwhelmed by the mountain of research on cancer treatments. Every day, she faced the tough job of going through countless studies to find the best options for her patients. One day, she discovered an AI-driven platform that analyzed patient data along with research findings. This amazing tool helped her make quick, informed decisions, allowing her to tailor treatment plans to fit each patient's needs.

After using the AI system, Dr. Harris noticed that patients with rare types of cancer were getting faster and more accurate treatment recommendations. The machine learning algorithms could spot patterns and connections in the data that might take a human years to figure out. One of her patients, a young mother named Claire, had been diagnosed with a rare form of leukemia. Thanks to AI, Dr. Harris found a groundbreaking clinical trial specifically for patients like Claire. With the timely insights from the AI, Claire was able to begin treatment just in time to celebrate her daughter's second birthday. In the face of challenges, AI became a shining beacon of hope, lighting the way through what once felt like a dark path.

The stories of AI's life-saving impacts don't stop there. Advances in personalized medicine are growing as AI systems analyze genetic profiles to predict how different patients will respond to specific treatments. This approach has the potential to change the game in fighting diseases that were previously difficult to treat. AI is more than just a tool for medical professionals; it acts as a partner in the healing process, working tirelessly to boost human capabilities and pave the way for a brighter future.

Shifting our focus to education, the powerful influence of AI continues to shine. Classrooms, which were once known for their one-size-fits-all approach, are transforming into vibrant learning environments where AI tools engage students in new and exciting ways.

Meet Omar, a high school student who struggled with math. Despite his best efforts, he often lagged behind his classmates, feeling discouraged and disconnected. But then his school rolled out an AI-driven tutoring program that adjusted to each student's pace and learning style. Omar found himself paired with a virtual tutor that broke down tough equations into simple steps. The AI platform identified his weak points and provided personalized exercises that gradually built his confidence.

As time went on, Omar not only improved in math but also developed a love for learning. The technology allowed him to explore the subject at his own speed, catering to his specific needs. Teachers also benefited; AI offered insights that helped them adjust their teaching strategies to ensure every student had the support they needed. This shift in education shows how AI can make learning more inclusive and accessible for all students, regardless of their backgrounds.

Moreover, AI's reach goes beyond individual learning experiences. Schools are using data analytics to identify trends, which helps them implement changes that encourage equity and inclusiveness. AI-driven dashboards allow administrators to see where resources are needed most, ensuring that every student gets the help they require to succeed. In this light, the future of education isn't just about technology; it's about cultivating an environment that promotes growth and opportunity for everyone.

Looking at the environmental challenges we face, it's clear that AI is also stepping up to tackle some of the biggest issues of our time. With climate change posing a serious threat to our planet, innovative AI solutions are being developed to guide us toward sustainability.

Consider a group of researchers working in a busy city. They used AI algorithms to analyze energy consumption patterns, uncovering inefficiencies that had been overlooked for years. By optimizing energy use across various sectors—homes, businesses, and industries—they significantly reduced the city's carbon footprint. The AI also provided real-time data on energy usage, helping residents and businesses make smarter choices about their consumption.

There are also inspiring stories of AI predicting natural disasters, offering early warnings that save lives. One initiative used machine learning to analyze satellite images and historical data to create algorithms that predict flood risks in vulnerable areas. When a storm was expected to hit a coastal town, the AI alerted local officials, enabling them to evacuate people and mobilize resources ahead of time. By integrating AI into environmental management, we see how technology and nature can work together for a healthier, more sustainable future.

Lucas Hartwell

Looking at the environmental challenges we face, it's clear that AI is also stepping up to tackle some of the biggest issues of our time. With climate change posing a serious threat to our planet, innovative AI solutions are being developed to guide us toward sustainability.

Consider a group of researchers working in a busy city. They used AI algorithms to analyze energy consumption patterns, uncovering inefficiencies that had been overlooked for years. By optimizing energy use across various sectors—homes, businesses, and industries—they significantly reduced the city's carbon footprint. The AI also provided real-time data on energy usage, helping residents and businesses make smarter choices about their consumption.

There are also inspiring stories of AI predicting natural disasters, offering early warnings that save lives. One initiative used machine learning to analyze satellite images and historical data to create algorithms that predict flood risks in vulnerable areas. When a storm was expected to hit a coastal town, the AI alerted local officials, enabling them to evacuate people and mobilize resources ahead of time. By integrating AI into environmental management, we see how technology and nature can work together for a healthier, more sustainable future.

school rolled out an AI-driven tutoring program that adjusted to each student's pace and learning style. Omar found himself paired with a virtual tutor that broke down tough equations into simple steps. The AI platform identified his weak points and provided personalized exercises that gradually built his confidence.

As time went on, Omar not only improved in math but also developed a love for learning. The technology allowed him to explore the subject at his own speed, catering to his specific needs. Teachers also benefited; AI offered insights that helped them adjust their teaching strategies to ensure every student had the support they needed. This shift in education shows how AI can make learning more inclusive and accessible for all students, regardless of their backgrounds.

Moreover, AI's reach goes beyond individual learning experiences. Schools are using data analytics to identify trends, which helps them implement changes that encourage equity and inclusiveness. AI-driven dashboards allow administrators to see where resources are needed most, ensuring that every student gets the help they require to succeed. In this light, the future of education isn't just about technology; it's about cultivating an environment that promotes growth and opportunity for everyone.

As we consider these promising developments, it's essential to keep a balanced view. The potential of AI is immense, but it also brings important challenges. Concerns about ethics, bias, and privacy are top of mind in conversations about AI. However, it's crucial to see that these challenges don't overshadow the hope that real-world applications can bring.

Hope isn't just about not feeling despair; it's an active force that inspires us to envision a future where technology and human values go hand in hand. Stories of people like Dr. Harris, Omar, and dedicated environmental researchers remind us of the positive impact AI can have when used thoughtfully. We must foster a mindset that acknowledges the pitfalls while also searching for opportunities to innovate and improve.

At this important moment, we're invited to rethink our relationship with technology. Instead of seeing AI as a threat, let's embrace it as a partner in creating a brighter future. Together, we can use the power of artificial intelligence to build a world where healthcare is accessible, education is tailored to individual needs, and our environment is protected for future generations. The challenges we face are not impossible; they are a call to innovate, inspire, and ignite change. As we move forward, let's hold onto the vision of a future where technology and humanity thrive together, driven by our shared commitment to making the world a better place for everyone.

Action Steps

As we look ahead to a future shaped by artificial intelligence, you might wonder how you can get involved in this exciting story. While hope is a powerful motivator, it's important that we also take real steps to engage with the world of AI. The possibilities for positive change are vast, but they require all of us to pitch in. So let's dive into how we can become informed advocates and active participants in crafting the future of technology.

First and foremost, education is the backbone of getting involved with AI. It's crucial for everyone to deepen their understanding of this fascinating field—not just to keep up with tech trends, but also to think critically about the ethical questions that come with them. Whether you're a student, a working professional, or just someone curious about what's going on in the world, there are countless resources available to help you boost your AI knowledge.

You might want to check out online courses from platforms like Coursera, edX, or Udacity. These sites offer great introductions to the basics of AI and even explore its impact on society. Many of these courses come from top universities and organizations, so you can access quality education from anywhere with an internet connection. Local community centers or universities often host workshops where you can learn directly from experts while connecting with others. Remember, learning shouldn't stop after one course; it's a journey that should continue as you explore the world of AI.

Look for local AI meetups or online discussion groups where people come together to talk about technology's impact on our lives. Connecting with others who share your interests can spark new ideas and encourage teamwork. Websites like Meetup.com or LinkedIn have groups focused on tech discussions that can be great for dialogue and sharing insights. By joining these communities, you not only expand your understanding of AI but also hear different viewpoints on its effects, which is vital in a diverse society.

Getting involved in your community is another fantastic way to take action. Knowledge is most beneficial when it's shared. By starting or joining local conversations about AI, you can help bridge the gap between complicated tech concepts and everyday life. Town hall meetings, community panels, or even casual get-togethers can be perfect venues for raising questions and voicing concerns about AI's role in our world.

Imagine organizing a community panel where experts talk about how AI affects healthcare, education, and the environment. Invite local educators, healthcare workers, and tech enthusiasts to share their insights, and allow time for questions and discussions. This setup creates a two-way conversation where community members can express their thoughts while also gaining valuable info. Not only does this build a sense of community, but it also encourages informed discussions about the future we want to create together.

In our social media-driven age, online discussion groups offer another avenue to engage with AI topics. Platforms like Reddit or Facebook host many groups focused on technology and its social implications. Jump into discussions, pose questions, and share your views on how AI is influencing your life and local community. The beauty of this digital era is that it connects us with people all over the world, building a lively community of curious minds eager to chat about the future of technology.

Advocacy is one of the most impactful actions anyone can take to shape the future of AI. As members of society, we have both the right and responsibility to call for transparency and ethical standards in AI development. This isn't just about voicing concerns; it's about holding developers and policymakers accountable. Writing to your local representatives about your thoughts on AI laws and ethical practices is a vital step. When officials hear from their constituents, it strengthens the conversation and encourages them to take action.

To make this easier, think about writing templates for letters or emails that clearly communicate your concerns and ideas. Be sure to personalize each note to reflect your true feelings and experiences. While it may feel overwhelming, remember that every little effort adds up to the bigger conversation. Organizations focused on responsible AI practices often welcome support too. Take the time to research and connect with these groups to learn about their missions and explore ways you can help.

Besides writing to representatives, speaking with policymakers in settings like town halls or public forums can amplify your voice. These gatherings offer a unique chance to share your perspective directly and sway decision-makers. Whenever possible, join discussions about AI regulation and ethics and present your views on the importance of using technology responsibly.

Cultivating a curious and critical mindset is key to joining the ongoing conversation about AI. Ask yourself questions about the technologies you come across every day. What algorithms are at work when you scroll through social media? How do AI systems influence the ads you see? By embracing this inquisitive attitude, you become an informed consumer who understands the implications of technology and actively engages in discussions about its path forward.

Encouraging a culture of inquiry is crucial, as it inspires others to think critically about the technologies in their lives. Share your curiosity with friends and family, engage in conversations about the ethical aspects of AI, and challenge common assumptions. This type of dialogue not only educates those around you but also builds a community of thinkers dedicated to using technology responsibly.

AI isn't just a buzzword; it's shaping our everyday experiences often without us realizing it. To navigate this landscape effectively, we need to stay aware of its developments and implications. Embrace chances to learn more about AI through reading books, attending lectures, or following thought leaders on social media. This ongoing engagement will keep you informed about new technologies and the ethical debates that come with them.

As we move ahead in a world increasingly influenced by AI, let's remember that everyone has a role to play. Education, community involvement, advocacy, and curiosity are the building blocks of responsible participation in this technological evolution. By taking action, we can work together toward a future where AI benefits humanity in positive and ethical ways.

The path to responsible AI engagement isn't just about what each of us can do individually; it's also about building a community committed to informed advocacy and critical thinking. Let's not just be passive consumers of technology; let's actively participate in shaping the future we want. Every action, no matter how small, contributes to a larger movement for a more ethical, transparent, and responsible tech landscape. Together, we can create a world where AI enhances our lives while honoring our core values and ethics.

In this light, the power of our collective voice is significant. When informed individuals unite to advocate for responsible AI practices, they can create meaningful change that influences laws, corporate practices, and societal norms. This collective effort is vital in ensuring that AI development aligns with human values and ethical standards.

As you think about the steps you can take, consider your passions and interests. What excites you about AI? What worries you? Let these reflections guide your involvement. Whether it's joining community discussions or pushing for policy changes, your voice is important. By stepping into your role, you can help cultivate a future where technology acts as a force for good instead of a source of division or harm.

Ultimately, our journey into an AI-enhanced future offers a unique chance for growth, dialogue, and collaboration. Let's take advantage of this moment to spark curiosity, promote community involvement, and advocate for ethical practices in AI development. By actively joining this conversation, we can move toward a future that truly reflects our shared values and dreams. Together, we can ensure that artificial intelligence becomes not just a tool for technological progress but a partner in our quest for a better, fairer world.

Our Shared Destiny

In the rich landscape of our everyday lives, few inventions are as influential as artificial intelligence. From the first moments we wake up and check our smartphones to the winding down of our day spent binge-watching beloved shows, AI quietly shapes our daily routines. It's woven into how we think about personal privacy, impacting everything from the way we shop online to how we connect with each other. The effects of AI go beyond individual experiences; they deeply influence the economy, labor markets, and social norms that define our shared existence. This connection highlights a shared destiny that we all play a role in shaping.

At its heart, AI is a powerful tool that has the potential to enrich our lives in many ways. However, its true power comes from the intentions, choices, and ethical guidelines set by those who create and use it. Each line of code carries the creator's views, values, and biases, leading us to an important question: Are we, as a society, ready to thoughtfully engage with this power? The answer isn't just about knowing the technology; it's also about including different voices in this important conversation. Many communities have often found themselves sidelined when it comes to technology advancements. To ensure everyone has a voice in the future of AI, we need to focus on inclusivity and representation as core values in its development.

When we welcome a variety of perspectives, we enrich the conversations surrounding AI and pave the way for innovations that truly benefit a wider range of people. Just imagine the possibilities that arise when individuals from diverse backgrounds—whether related to race, gender, economic status, or geographic location—come together to create AI solutions. The outcome could be technologies that not only meet the needs of the majority but also uplift the voices of those often unheard. Initiatives that empower underrepresented groups should be central to our collective mission. Programs providing education, mentorship, and resources in technology can help break down barriers and unlock new paths for these communities.

For example, organizations dedicated to closing the tech education gap play a crucial role in this effort. They offer training in areas like data science, coding, and machine learning to individuals who might not have access to such resources otherwise. By empowering these individuals, we can spark a new wave of innovation that reflects the unique experiences and viewpoints of our diverse society. When those who have traditionally been excluded step into active roles in AI development, we foster an environment that emphasizes human welfare and ethical considerations.

The idea of shared destiny goes beyond individuals and communities; it includes collaborative frameworks that bring together tech companies, governments, and civil society organizations to pursue ethical AI. The challenges posed by AI are too complex for anyone to tackle alone. By forming successful partnerships, we can encourage innovation while prioritizing human well-being. Imagine a tech company teaming up with local governments to create AI systems that improve public services, like transportation or healthcare, while addressing the specific needs of the community. This kind of teamwork shows how shared goals and resources can lead to meaningful progress.

Consider the recent partnerships aimed at promoting ethical AI practices. In various cities around the world, local governments have joined forces with tech companies to create guidelines for AI use in public safety. These collaborations include input from the community, ensuring that local voices help shape the policies that impact their lives. Such efforts not only foster transparency but also build trust between the public and technology developers. When communities see that their concerns are acknowledged and valued, they are more likely to welcome technological advancements rather than feel anxious about them.

Moreover, successful collaborations often bring about innovative solutions that focus on inclusivity. For instance, a project that uses AI to identify and reduce bias in hiring can lead to fairer workplaces. Involving diverse stakeholders in the creation and implementation of technology makes sure the resulting solutions are sensitive to the unique aspects of various demographics. Taking this proactive approach is crucial in crafting AI that serves the greater good.

As we reflect on our shared destiny, let's imagine a future where AI serves as a partner in progress. We need to inspire each other to envision the amazing things we can achieve when technology is built with humanity at its core. By looking toward a future shaped by values of collaboration and inclusivity, we can nurture a culture of innovation that is both responsible and aspirational.

In this environment, the potential for AI to be a force for good is huge. However, this vision relies on our collective responsibility to chart its course. Each of us has a role to play in shaping our technological future. Whether through community advocacy, engaging in discussions about AI ethics, or simply exploring educational resources, we have the power to influence how AI develops and fits into our lives.

Imagine a world where AI systems aim not only for profits but also to enhance our quality of life. Picture smart algorithms that prioritize sustainability, reduce inequality, and promote wellness. This vision isn't just a dream; it can become a reality through collective efforts that blend diverse viewpoints and collaborative frameworks. As we shoulder this responsibility, we must remind ourselves that the future of AI isn't set in stone. Instead, it's a blank canvas waiting for us to paint our shared vision, guided by our common values.

The call to action reaches everyone, encouraging a shift in mindset towards responsibility and agency. This isn't just about seeing AI as a tool; it's about recognizing it as a reflection of our shared hopes for society. By staying engaged, advocating for transparency, and demanding ethical standards, we can hold developers and policymakers accountable to ensure the technology we create aligns with our core principles.

As we stand on the threshold of this technological revolution, let's create an atmosphere where curiosity, critical thinking, and inclusivity flourish. Let's build spaces—both online and in our communities—where open discussions about the impact of AI can thrive. When we share our thoughts and ideas, we enrich the conversation and inspire others to join in. The journey toward a responsible AI landscape is a shared one; it requires contributions from every corner of society.

In this light, consider the impact of your voice. The future of AI development isn't just the responsibility of tech experts. Instead, it's shaped by an entire ecosystem of people who care deeply about how technology interacts with humanity. You have the ability to influence your community, advocate for ethical practices, and contribute to a narrative that emphasizes the common good.

As we envision a future where AI coexists with humanity, let's embrace the notion that our destinies are interconnected. The choices we make today will resonate for generations to come. By grappling with the complexities of AI development and advocating for a shared vision of humanity, we can create a world where technology enhances our strengths and addresses our vulnerabilities.

To nurture this shared destiny, we can use various platforms that encourage dialogue and teamwork. Social media, community forums, and public discussions are great ways to share ideas and perspectives. These interactions not only create opportunities for learning but also empower individuals to take an active role in shaping the narrative around AI and its effects on society.

Think about the power of storytelling in this context. Sharing personal stories and insights can highlight the human side of technology. When people talk about their experiences with AI—be they positive or negative—it adds depth to the conversation and encourages others to reflect on their own experiences. This sharing can spark change, prompting discussions that could lead to improvements in both AI design and implementation.

As we get closer to realizing a future shaped by AI, let's stay committed to inclusivity and ethical practices. The road ahead may be filled with obstacles, but together, we can navigate these challenges. By actively participating in ongoing discussions about AI, we can help pave the way for a future where innovation and human values exist side by side.

Ultimately, envisioning AI as a partner in progress starts with us. It calls for engagement, responsibility, and a united commitment to ensuring that technology enhances our human experience rather than detracts from it. Together, we can dream of a future where artificial intelligence shines as a beacon of hope, lighting the way toward a better world, one where our collective efforts forge a legacy of empowerment, inclusivity, and ethical growth.

Lucas Hartwell

Conclusion

As we close the pages of "Probability of Doom," we find ourselves at a crossroads. The journey through the landscape of artificial intelligence has revealed a future brimming with possibility, yet fraught with challenges. We've seen how AI can revolutionize healthcare, transform education, and tackle global issues like climate change. But we've also confronted the stark realities of job displacement, privacy concerns, and the potential for AI systems to perpetuate societal biases.

The future of AI isn't set in stone—it's a canvas we're all painting together. Each of us has a role to play in shaping this technology's trajectory. Whether you're a policymaker, a developer, or simply a concerned citizen, your voice matters in this ongoing dialogue.

The probability of doom isn't a foregone conclusion—it's a challenge we can meet with wisdom, empathy, and collective action. The future of AI is in our hands. Let's build it responsibly, together.

Lucas Hartwell

www.ingramcontent.com/pod-product-compliance
Lightning Source LLC
Chambersburg PA
CBHW052155220526
45471CB00004B/1690